J. M Boland

The Problem of Methodism :

Being a Review of the Residue Theory of Regeneration and the Second...

J. M Boland

The Problem of Methodism :
Being a Review of the Residue Theory of Regeneration and the Second...

ISBN/EAN: 9783337086343

Printed in Europe, USA, Canada, Australia, Japan

Cover: Foto ©Thomas Meinert / pixelio.de

More available books at **www.hansebooks.com**

THE
PROBLEM OF METHODISM:

Being a Review of the Residue Theory of Regeneration and the Second Change Theory of Sanctification; and the Philosophy of Christian Perfection.

BY THE REV. J. M. BOLAND, A.M.,

Author of "A Bible View of Baptism."

"Where sin abounded, grace did much more abound."—*St. Paul.*

J. D. BARBEE, AGENT.
PUBLISHING HOUSE OF THE M. E. CHURCH, SOUTH.
PRINTED FOR THE AUTHOR.
NASHVILLE, TENN.
1888.

Entered, according to Act of Congress, in the year 1888,
BY J. M. BOLAND,
in the Office of the Librarian of Congress, at Washington.

PREFACE.

The following treatise is the result of years of investigation. The conclusions which we have adopted are the most reasonable and scriptural solution of the difficult problem involved. If there be those who can not accept our views, we shall think none the less of them for it. We claim the right to *think* and *investigate*, and we accord the same to others. If any man has any new light to shed upon the problem we have discussed, let him speak in the fear of God and the love of the truth, and we will hear him patiently. As *truth* is the pearl we prize above rubies, if we are in error we are ready to receive new light. We are not so shut up to our views but that we are ready to adopt any theory of the divine life which is more reasonable and scriptural than the one we have adopted.

Our object is not to lower the standard of Christian experience, but to remove some of the confusion which has gathered around it, and place it where the inspired writers left it.

While we have called in question some *opinions*

of our standard authors, yet our views quadrate with our Articles of Faith, and are in harmony with our Standards so far as they are in harmony with themselves. We allow no one to esteem our standard authors more highly than we do, but we do not believe that they are infallible any more than the Pope of Rome. If we did not believe that we have thrown new light on some points we would not offer another book on this often investigated subject; but believing this, this volume is sent forth on its mission by the AUTHOR.

INTRODUCTION.

Dr. Thornwell truly says: "We love opinions instead of truth. Education becomes second nature—the dogmas of the one are mistaken for the instructions of the other. So we quietly accept as intuitively obvious, that which we learned in the nursery—hence, error is perpetuated from age to age. One generation transmits a large legacy of errors to another; and the dream of tranquillity is not disturbed until some emergency arises, which compels examination and enforces inquiry."

But even then, the world is slow to give up long-received opinions. Every new idea advanced is weighed and criticised to see if it agrees with preconceived opinions, instead of trying it by the standard of reason and the word of God. Though Luther and Melanchthon succeeded in breaking loose from the leading errors of Romanism, they did not live long enough to give to the world a system of doctrine complete and harmonious in every part. A work of such magnitude as the Reformation could not easily be accomplished in one generation. The errors of the "Dark Ages" were many, deep, and radical. But, by the aid of science and a more thorough study of the Bible, many of the tenets in that stupendous compilation called Orthodoxy have been modified; as time moved on new errors were discovered, exposed, and finally renounced; and still the work is not done.

My idea is that we make a mistake in calling any of our systems orthodox—even the best of them. They are all imperfect; they all contain error—perhaps a good deal of it. In making up our Creed, we ought to start with the idea of choosing between imperfect orthodoxies, and not between one orthodoxy and a hundred heterodoxies; then take the one which on the whole presents the fewest difficulties and fits the largest number of ascertained facts. I would not dare to frame a form of words, however clear to my mind, and say to another man: Accept this, or you are not orthodox. "The Lord has more truth yet to break out of his holy word." I can not sufficiently bewail the condition of those who have come to a period in religion. Luther, Calvin, and Knox, great and good and wise and learned; Arminius, Wesley, and Watson, also great and good and wise and learned: is it high *treason* to say of any of them and all of them, "These penetrated not into the whole counsel of God?" With every discussion there has been real progress. More comprehensive and precise statements, as well as clearer conceptions, have been attained up to the present day. In the future progress will largely depend upon our liberality in considering opinions which vary from the current and accepted orthodoxy, and also upon our vigor and boldness in resisting the error we may discover in such opinions. So let us help one another, and God will guide us into all truth. Then we shall all be orthodox.

CONTENTS.

Chapter I.
A General Survey of the Subject.................. 11

Chapter II.
The Twofold Nature of Man...................... 34

Chapter III.
"Sin in Believers.".................................... 69

Chapter IV.
"How Readest Thou?"............................. 97

Chapter V.
The Modern Fathers in Trouble................... 131

Chapter VI.
"Regeneration a Partial Renovation.".......... 158

Chapter VII.
Christian Perfection................................. 191

Chapter VIII.
"Not Under the Law, but Under Grace."...... 223

Chapter IX.
The Laws and Conditions of Spiritual Growth. 249

Chapter X.
The Christian's Secret of a Happy Life......... 281

Chapter XI.
"Now of the Things of Which We Have Spoken, This Is the Sum.".................... 308

The Problem of Methodism.

CHAPTER I.

A General Survey of the Subject.

THE mission of Methodism is to "spread scriptural holiness over these lands." Mr. Wesley says: "My brother Charles and I, reading the Bible, saw we could not be saved without holiness; we followed after it and incited others so to do. . . . Holiness was our object—inward and outward holiness. . . God then thrust us out to raise up a holy people." "This doctrine (inward and outward holiness) is the grand depositum which God has lodged with the people called Methodists; and for the sake of propagating this doctrine he appears to have raised us up."

In writing to his brother Charles, Mr. Wesley says: "Insist everywhere on full salvation received now by faith. Press the instantaneous blessing." Again he says: "Let all our preachers make a point of preaching perfection to believers, constantly, strongly, explicitly. . . . I am afraid Christain perfection will be forgotten. A general faintness in this respect has fallen on the whole kingdom. Sometimes I seem almost weary of striving against the stream of both preachers and people." He wrote to Dr. Clarke thus: "To retain the grace of God is much more than to gain it. And this should be strongly urged on all who have tasted of perfect love. If you can prove that any of our preachers or leaders, either directly or **indirectly,** speak against it, **let him be a** preacher **or** a leader no longer. I doubt whether he should continue **in the** Society. **Because** he that could **thus speak in our** congregation **cannot be an honest man."**

Dr. **Clarke says: " If Methodists give up preaching entire** sanctification **they will** soon lose their **glory.** . . . Let **all** those who retain **the** apostolic doctrine, **that 'the blood of** Jesus Christ cleanseth from all sin,' press every believer to go on to perfection and expect to be saved while **here** below, unto **the** fullness **of** the blessing of **the gospel of** Christ."

Bishop Asbury says: **"I am divinely** impressed with **a charge to** preach sanctification **in every sermon."**

Bishop McKendree wrote to the seraphic Summerfield thus: " But superior to all these I trust you will ever keep in view, in all your ministrations, the great design which we believe God intended to accomplish in the world, in making us 'a people that were not a people.' I mean the knowledge, not of a free and a present, but also a full salvation—in other words, a salvation from all sin unto all holiness. Insist much on this; build up the Churches herein, and proclaim aloud that 'without holiness no man shall see the Lord.' Under the guidance of the Spirit of Holiness, this doctrine will be acknowledged of God; signs will follow them that believe and press after this uttermost salvation, and our people will bear the mark of their high-calling, become a holy nation, a peculiar people."

In addition to these individual utterances, the Bishops in their quadrennial addresses, and the General Conferences in their pastoral addresses to the whole Church, "have, at various periods, sent forth the most unequivocal and emphatic deliverances."

In their quadrennial address to the General Conference of 1824, the Bishops said: "Do we, as preachers, feel the same child-like spirit which so eminently distinguished our first ministers? Do we come to the people in the fullness of the blessing of the gospel of peace? . . . Are we striving by faith and obedience to elevate our hearts and lives to the standard of gospel holiness? or are we wishing to have the standard lowered to our unsanctified natures? In short, are we content to have the doctrine of Christian holiness an article of our Creed only, without becoming experimentally and practically acquainted with it? Are we pressing after it as the prize of our high calling in Christ Jesus? . . . If the Methodists lose sight of this doctrine they will fall by their own weight. Their success in gaining members will be the cause of their dissolution. Holiness is the main cord that binds us together. Relax this and you loosen the whole system. . . . The original design of Methodism was to raise up and preserve a holy people. This was the principal object which Mr. Wesley had in view. To this end all the doctrines believed and preached by the Methodists tend. Whoever supposed, or who that is acquainted with the case, can suppose it was designed, in any of its parts, to secure the applause and popularity of the world, or a numerical increase of worldly or impenitent men? Is there any provision made for the aggrandizement of our ministers or the worldly-mindedness of our members? None whatever!"

In 1832 the General Conference issued a pastoral address to the whole Church, in which they said: "When we speak of holiness we mean that state in which God is loved with all the heart and served with all our powers. This, as Methodists, we have said, is the privilege of the Christian in this life. . . . Is it not time, in this matter, to return to first principles? Is it not time that we throw off the inconsistency with which we are charged in regard to this matter? . . . And when this shall come to pass we may expect a corresponding increase of Christian enjoyment, and in the force of religious influence we shall exert over others."

Passing by many more documents of

this kind from which we might quote, we come to the Centennial Conference of American Methodism, which met in Baltimore in 1884, and which re-affirmed the faith of the Church in all its branches, in these words: "We remind you, brethren, that the mission of Methodism is to promote holiness. This end and aim enters into all our organic life. Holiness is the fullness of life, the crown of the soul, the joy and strength of the Church. It is not a sentiment or an emotion, but a principle inwrought in the heart, the culmination of God's work in us followed by a consecrated life."

Thus an earnest desire for Bible Holiness drew together in Christian sympathy and finally organized that band of godly men which were first called the "Holy Club," then "Methodists."

As they said themselves, they banded together to "seek inward and outward holiness." They "hungered and thirsted after righteousness." They groaned to be "cleansed from all sin," and to be "filled with all the fullness of God." So they "organized class-meetings, where they might open their hearts one to another, and tell their conflicts and triumphs, their joys and sorrows, and thus mutually stimulate and assist." They met in foundries and workshops and in the open air to pray and sing and exhort. In love-feasts they told of their growth in grace and of their yearnings after holiness of heart and life. They were filled and ruled by one supreme, overmastering desire to be holy themselves and urge others to the same experience. They preached it, prayed for it, professed it, sung of it, illustrated it in their lives, and died testifying "The blood of Jesus Christ his Son cleanseth from all unrighteousness." And when this band of devout souls "crystallized into a Church," it was for the expressed purpose of elevating Christian experience, reviving primitive Christianity, and of "spreading scriptural holiness over the land." And so they adopted the "General Rules" of Mr. Wesley's "United Societies" as their "conception of Bible religion, affirming that all these rules are taught of God in his written word, which is the only rule and the sufficient rule of our faith and practice. And all these we know his Spirit writes on truly awakened hearts."

In keeping with all this, we call attention to the fact that the vows of Church-membership demand a complete consecration: "Dost thou renounce the devil and all his works—the vain pomp and glory of the world, with all covetous desires of the same, and the carnal desires of the flesh, so that thou wilt not follow or be led by them? Answer: I renounce them all. Wilt thou then obediently keep God's holy will and commandments, and walk in the same all the days of thy life? Answer: I will endeavor so to do, God being my helper." Thus a complete surrender was demanded of each applicant at the very threshold of the Church; none were invited to join unless he had a fixed "desire to flee from the wrath to come, and to be *saved from his sins.*"

When ministers were to be set apart in this Church, "these spiritually-minded fathers" said: "Let the following questions be asked: Do they know God as a pardoning God? Have they the love of God abiding in them? Do they desire nothing but God? Are they *holy* in all manner of conversation?" When, after sufficient trial, these preachers were brought forward to be received into the Annual Conference, and appointed regular pastors over the flock, they were asked the following questions —viz.: "Have you faith in Christ? Do you expect to be made perfect in love in this life? Are you groaning after it? Are you resolved to devote yourself wholly to God and his work?" In these questions, and the answers given, the mind and purpose of the Methodist Church are clearly defined. Raised up, as she was, to "spread scriptural holiness over these lands," she has always refused to ordain any preacher who was indifferent on the subject of Bible holiness.

Here, then, we find the central purpose and inspiration of Methodism. It is Primitive Christianity revived— "Christianity in earnest"—"Christ in you the hope of glory:" "whom we preach, warning every man, and teaching every man in all wisdom; that we may present every man perfect in Christ Jesus." "Methodism is for Bible holiness, or it is for nothing. Take that out of our preaching and it is emasculated. Take that out of your living and you have nothing left worth your time and effort!"

If we turn to the Bible we find holiness taught, holiness commanded, holiness offered, holiness attainable, holiness already attained and enjoyed. If "Christ gave himself for us that he might redeem us from all iniquity, and purify unto himself a peculiar people, zealous of good works," then we may be "*purified*" and become a " peculiar people." If " Christ died without the gate that he might sanctify the people with his own blood," then the people may be "*sanctified*" and " preserved *blameless* until the coming of the Lord Jesus." If " Christ also loved the Church, and gave himself for it; that he might sanctify and cleanse it, and present it to himself a glorious Church, not having spot, or wrinkle, or any such thing; but that it should be holy and without blemish," then the Church may be "*holy, not having spot, or wrinkle, or blemish, or any such thing!*" To assume any thing less than this is to cast contempt on the provisions of grace, and to limit and dishonor the vicarious death of Christ! Holiness is the great truth that glows on every page of revelation, and webs its way all through the Bible. It sparkles, and whispers, and sings, and shouts, in all its prophecy, and biography, and poetry, and promises, and prayers! No wonder, then, that John and Charles Wesley concluded "from reading the Bible," that they "could not be saved without holiness." The truth is, all who read the Bible as the word of God are led to the same conclusion. Even the Church of Rome, with all her corruptions and abominations and perversions of Scripture, found it easier to invent a purgatory in which to purify the soul, than to set aside the grand Bible doctrine, "without holiness no man shall see the Lord." And if there is a Church on earth which does not hold and teach that holiness is necessary to get to heaven, I have never heard of it. The only controversy among the Churches is in regard to the time, the place, and the means by which the work is done. Methodism stands alone among all the Churches, in preaching a *present salvation from all* sin, *by faith in the blood of the Lamb, and the possibility* of such a one " *abiding in Christ and sinning not.*"

Now, while every branch of Methodism stands pledged to preach a present salvation from all sin, to be followed by a life of holiness, yet it is a lamentable fact that from John Wesley to the present there have been two theories of the divine life shut up in the womb of Methodism; and, like Esau and Jacob, they have "struggled together." While John Wesley did more than any other man to revive primitive Christianity and to clear up the muddy theology of the Dark Ages, yet it is a remarkable fact that he failed to harmonize his theory of the divine life at some points; "and what shall the man do that cometh after the king?" The modern Methodist fathers and authors, who adopted Mr. Wesley's theory, have not only failed to harmonize Mr. Wesley with himself, but they have "found no end in wandering mazes lost." If the reader thinks these are strong statements, we plead guilty, for we weighed every word in order to make them strong; but if he thinks they are too strong, then we ask him to suspend his final judgment until he has read these pages through.

The great mistake Mr. Wesley made was in adopting the "residue theory of regeneration" and the "second change theory of sanctification." The next mistake was in confounding "sanctification with Christian perfection." This mistake has done a deal of harm. Take any theory of sanctification you please —let it be a first, second, third, or fourth blessing; but do not confound sanctification with Christian perfection. Sanctification is moral *purity;* perfection is Christian *maturity.* The one is the result of an act of cleansing; the other is the result of a growth in grace. The one is done in a moment; the other is the work of time and experience. The newborn soul *may* be *pure,* but he *cannot* be *mature.*

After reading every book on the subject I could obtain, after consulting every text of scripture quoted, I have reached this conclusion: Regeneration is a complete work in its nature, and *includes* sanctification, or moral purity, while Christian perfection is a state of freedom from sin, and includes a maturity of the Christian graces. The one is instantaneous and complete, admitting of no degrees; the other is progressive—a growth, a going on, until the full stature of a perfect man in Christ is reached. Holiness and perfect love will fit into this theory, at the proper place, as we proceed.

The Ninth Article of the Church of England declares that "original sin is the corruption of the nature of every man; . . . and this *infection of nature doth remain in them that are regenerated.*" As Mr. Wesley belonged to this Church, and wrote from the stand-point of this Ninth Article, we can see how he came to adopt the residue theory of regeneration; and then he had to give up the doctrine of sanctification, or else bring in sanctification as a "second change" to get rid of this "remaining corruption." But, as Mr. Wesley cut this objectionable clause out of the Articles of Faith which he prepared for the Methodist Episcopal Church in America, it is a little strange that so many American Methodists adopted the residue theory of regeneration.

In reading up on this subject, I have been amazed to see how this theory of the divine life has led men to *minify* regeneration and *magnify* sanctification. Take a few examples: "The carnal mind survives the work of regeneration, and is often actively rebellious in the hearts of real Christians." "In this regenerate state, the former corruptions of the heart may remain and strive for the mastery." "Although in regeneration holy principles are infused into the soul, yet the *change produced is only partial.*" "As long as Christians live in a *partially* purified state," etc. "The new life has existence in a soul *partially carnal* in the *mere* regenerate." "Regeneration removes *some sin or pollution,* and entire sanctification removes the corruption which remains after regeneration." "Regeneration consists simply in *partial renovation* and divine adoption."

Now I submit that any theory of the divine life that leads to such expressions as the above cannot be harmonized with the Bible idea of the "new birth," the "new man," and the "new creation." Hence, Mr. Wesley never did reconcile the residue theory with his own definition of the "new birth." I would like to see one of our modern "Holiness Conventions" harmonize the following utterances of Mr. Wesley:

1. "By all the grace given at justification, we

1. "To be born again, is to be *inwardly* changed

cannot wholly cleanse either our hearts or hands. Most sure we cannot, till it shall please our Lord to speak to our hearts again, to speak the second time, 'Be clean!' and then only, the leprosy is cleansed. Then only the carnal mind is destroyed, and inbred sin subsists no more."

2. "If there be no second change, no instantaneous deliverance after justification, then we must remain full of sin till death." "Certainly sanctification is an instantaneous deliverance from all sin."

from *all* sinfulness to *all* holiness." "He is created anew in Christ Jesus. He is washed, he is *sanctified*. His heart is *purified* by faith; he is cleansed from the corruption that is in the world." "That which is born of the Spirit is spiritual, heavenly, divine, like its author."

2. "Every one that hath Christ in him the hope of glory is saved from all sin, from all unrighteousness." "It is undeniably true that sanctification is a *progressive* work, carried on in the soul by slow degrees."

After reading the above deliverances, and many more of the same import, we are prepared to hear him say: "Perhaps I have an *exceedingly complex* idea of sanctification!"*

We propose to examine the residue theory of regeneration and the second change theory of sanctification, in the light of reason, psychology, and the Word of God. In order to explain those mental states which have been called "sin in believers," "inbred sin," the "remains of the carnal mind," the "corruption of our nature," the "body of sin," and the "old man," we must first discuss the twofold nature of man, the effects of the fall, and the philosophy of temptation.

---

* The only solution of this confusion is given in the last chapter of this book, to which we call special attention.

CHAPTER II.

The Twofold Nature of Man.

Every man—and of course every Christian—has at least two natures.* The one is designed to be subordinate and subservient to the other. Each has its office to fill—it takes both to constitute a *man;* and "the highest style of man" is he whose twofold nature is in

---

* The sharp psychomachy, which Paul so well portrays, interprets the consciousness of millions. That man is not all of the earth; that he is endowed with a higher nature, reaching to heaven, all Christians agree, and with them thousands who are not Christians coincide. In the minuter analysis of humanity, Dichotomists and Trichotomists contend, and many deeply interesting questions in Ontology and Psychology arise. These mysteries of humanity have bewildered theologians, and thereby troubled Christians.

harmony at once with itself and with the Creator.

In reference to the effects of the fall of man and the work of restoration through the gospel, there are two erroneous opinions or theories. The one is, that such is the condition of man's lower nature, since the fall, that it is impossible for him to live without committing sin daily. The other is, that all the lower affinities and sensibilities of our nature must be so crucified and destroyed that there will be no stirring of the emotions nor enkindling of the desires toward any forbidden object.

The first theory is supposed to be taught in the seventh chapter of Romans. But the character described there is a convicted Pharisee, and not a renewed and sanctified Christian. The new life and the Christian character are described in the eighth chapter of Romans. Moreover, John says: "Whosoever is born of God [and abideth in him] doth not commit sin."

The second theory is supposed to be set forth in the sixth chapter of Romans and other passages, where the Christian life is represented as a "crucifixion of the old man," and a "death of sin." Now the great object of the gospel is to give to our spiritual nature, which is "dead in sin," its true, original life, and through it to restore all the lower elements of our essential constitution to order and their proper functions, but not to destroy any of them. Dr. Clarke says: "The 'old man,' the 'body of sin,' is the same as the 'infection of our nature,' in consequence of the fall." Hence, the "old man," the "body of sin," must be "destroyed," but not the *nature* of man. The "*corruption* of our nature" must be removed, but all the essential elements of our twofold nature are left *intact*. When the "desires are drawn out and enticed" by an evil object, the desires must be "*rejected*" and thereby "*mortified*," but neither the *capacity* to desire, nor the *susceptibility* to feel the force of enticement to sin, are to be destroyed; for that would put man beyond the possibility of being tempted, which possibility must exist while probation continues.

Let us go to the very root of this subject. Without a clear view of man's essential nature, we are incompetent to judge of the correctness or defects of any theory of the divine life. If we wish to know what were the effects of the fall upon man's essential nature, and what is necessary to renew man's nature "in righteousness and true holiness," we must ascertain what that nature was as he came from the hand of his Creator. We learn from the Bible that man, while in a state of *innocence* and *purity*, was subjected to temptation; and that he possessed, then, appetites, emotions, and desires similar in nature to those belonging to the human mind and constitution now. "When the woman saw that the tree was good for food, and that it was pleasant to the eyes, and a tree to be desired to make one wise, she took of the fruit thereof and did eat." (Gen. iii. 6.) Here we have: first, a perception of a forbidden object; second, the appetite for food awakened; third, the emotions of pleasure stirred; fourth, the desire to know enkindled; and, finally, the volition and act that constituted the sin by which man fell.

It is clear, then, that man, in his best estate, possessed all those mental capacities called natural sensibilities, and that these sensibilities were susceptible of being addressed and excited by a forbidden object. Instead, then, of these natural sensibilities being, in some mysterious way, the result of the fall, they belong to and are inseparable from the human constitution in its original organization. Man, considered in the light of Biblical psychology, possessed them all in his pristine purity. But when he fell, those faculties which were essential to humanity became perverted and corrupted, and passions which were intended to perform only a subordinate part became controlling; but no new faculty was projected into his constitution. Whatever we may find in man's fallen, depraved nature to *purify* and regulate, we find no constitutional sensibilities to be obliterated, no faculty to be destroyed.

Depravity, then, is not a real *entity*, existing apart from man's essential constitution—not an actual *substance*, or real *entity*, projected into man's constitution; but a *corruption* and a *perversion* of man's essential powers. In the absence of *spiritual life*, the great controlling principle which was lost in the fall, man's moral nature is not only paralyzed, but all the lower elements of his essential nature transcend their true bounds and run riot in indulgence, so that "man is prone to go astray from his youth up." Now, this depravity is *personified* by Paul as the "old man," the "body of sin;" because man's higher nature is under the *dominion* of his lower nature. This depravity, this dominion of the flesh over the spirit, this "course of carnal thinking," Paul also calls "the carnal mind." Now this "course of carnal thinking," this "inherited tendency to sin," is what Paul calls "the law of sin and death," from which, he affirms, "the law of the Spirit of life in Christ Jesus makes us *free*." Hence, "to be carnally minded is [spiritual] death; but to be spiritually minded is life and peace." "Now if any man have not the Spirit of Christ, he is none of his;" and, "if so be that the Spirit of God dwell in you," then this "law of the Spirit of life in Christ Jesus hath made you free from the law of sin and death." How any man can read and study the sixth chapter of Romans, where Paul proves conclusively that the *normal* state of spiritual life presupposes a "crucifixion of the old man" and a "destruction of the body of sin" and a "death to sin," and then hold to the "residue theory of regeneration," is simply amazing! And how any man can read and study the eighth chapter of Romans, where Paul discusses the "carnal mind" and the "spiritually minded," and then say that "this carnal mind survives the work of regeneration, and is often actively *rebellious* in the hearts of real Christians," is a mystery that transcends the enigmatical philosophy of the Persians. To be able to expose such errors, and to explain those mental states relied on to prove them, we must investigate the laws that govern our twofold nature far enough to have a clear view of the mental states involved in the philosophy of temptation.

In all the discussions of the twofold

nature of man which I have seen, bearing on the "residue theory of regeneration," several important facts have been ignored or overlooked. The advancement that has been made in mental science, in some of its nicer distinctions, since Mr. Wesley's day, puts one on vantage-ground which he did not occupy, or he would have been shocked at the very thought of putting "*lust*" in the catalogue of "sin in believers;" for "*lust* is an *inordinate* desire," and no desire can become inordinate without the sympathy and assent of the will; and, therefore, wherever "lust" exists, its possessor has fallen into condemnation. (Matt. v. 28.) But to the ignored or overlooked facts. All standard authors on mental philosophy divide the sensibilities into two classes—natural and moral. Under the term "natural sensibilities" they speak of *natural* emotions and desires; and under the term "moral sensibilities" they speak of moral emotions and obligatory feelings.

Now, it is in the natural sensibilities that we find a class of mental states that connect us with the material and outer world, perception being the door of communication. These sensibilities, being *natural*, have no *moral* quality in themselves, but they form the *basis* of every solicitation to evil. The mind is so constituted that without the natural sensibilities—the natural emotions and desires—we cannot see how any man could be enticed to evil; but with these, we can see how even the Incarnate Son of God could be "tempted in all points like as we are," and how he could "suffer, being tempted."

As the natural sensibilities connect

us with the natural world, so the moral sensibilities connect us with the spiritual world; and these form the *basis* of all religion. In these we find man's capacity to be religious; and here is the region where the fall expended its blighting power. The effects of the fall upon the natural sensibilities may be accounted for largely in their excessive indulgence, growing out of the absence of a moral or spiritual power to control and direct them. But when we enter the moral nature of man, we find a picture answering to the one drawn by the pencil of inspiration to represent fallen, depraved humanity.

Now, as sin has done its fearful work in man's moral and spiritual nature, so here is the place for the work of restoration to be expected and the work of cleansing to be sought. We do not deny that the entire man will feel the effects of this restoration, when the soul is "renewed according to the divine pattern in righteousness and true holiness;" for this restores order to the mind, puts the will upon its throne, and gives it power to resist every solicitation to evil, and to "reject" and "mortify" the desires excited and drawn out toward forbidden objects. But to say that the natural sensibilities are to be so "crucified" as not to be stirred and enkindled by a pleasing or a desirable object, implies their utter destruction. To say that they may be dead to all evil but alive to all good will not remove the difficulty, for their being *natural* and not *moral* faculties makes no distinction—they are simply pleased at whatever is pleasing and desire whatever is desirable, and the moral faculties must detect the evil and the will reject the wrong.

This brings us to consider the mental states involved in temptation—a subject about which much has been written, and which is intimately connected with any theory of the divine life, but especially with the "residue theory of regeneration" and the "second change theory of sanctification." George Bell and Thomas Maxfield, who were the first of Mr. Wesley's lay preachers to profess sanctification as a "second change," soon professed to have become so holy as to be "free from temptation." These enthusiasts and their successors failed to see that probation implies trial, and trial implies temptation, and therefore temptation must exist as long as probation lasts.

But there are others who admit that

no state of grace in this life will free us from temptation, yet they so confound temptation and sin that they are constantly seeking exemption from the former under the name of the latter. These errorists have pressed the doctrine of self-crucifixion so far that, if they could live up to their theory, they would be incapable of feeling any solicitation to evil, and hence would be beyond the reach of temptation. The only way to clear up this confusion is to so analyze the mental states involved in temptation as to be able to locate the exact point at which temptation *ends* and sin *begins.*

Now there can be no temptation (in the sense of a solicitation to evil) unless the solicitation is brought ultimately to press upon the will. The will is the great umpire of the mind; and every solicitation to evil must come to this tribunal before it can be regarded a temptation. There are some preliminary steps; but there is a principle upon which the temptation presses—around which the force of the solicitation gathers and enters into contest—and that principle is the will.

Now we can only reach the will from without through perception, the natural emotions, and desires. For instance, a man perceives a forbidden object, which is pleasing to his natural sensibilities; this stirs his emotions and enkindles his desires, and the desires press upon the will for its concurrence; then, and not till then, does the solicitation become a temptation. The mental process in temptation, therefore, is from perception to emotions, from emotions to desires, and from desires to the will.

Let us compare this analysis of temptation with the Word of God: "And when the woman *saw* that the tree was good for food, and it was *pleasant* to the eyes, and a tree to be *desired* to make one wise, she *took* of the fruit thereof and *did eat*." (Gen. iii. 6.) Here we have the whole process, step by step, from perception to volition, of a successful temptation, and it agrees with our analysis in every particular.

In James i. 14, 15 we find the exact point where temptation ends and sin begins. We give Mr. Wesley's translation of this important text: "Every man is tempted when he is drawn away of his own desire and enticed [so far it is a temptation]. Then when desire hath conceived [gained the assent of the will] it bringeth forth sin." That is clear. The "man is tempted when he is drawn away of his own desire and enticed;" the solicitation, then, must be addressed to the will, or it is no temptation at all, and the will is reached through perception, the emotions, and the desires. It follows, then, that the stirrings of the emotions and the enkindlings of the desires, aside from the concurrence of the will, have no more moral quality than the pulsations of the heart. The one is the natural process for circulating the blood; the other is the natural process of a temptation. And yet a large class of good men so confound temptation with sin—the enkindlings of desire with the acts of the will—that every time they are severely tempted —"drawn away of their own desires and enticed"—they imagine that they have sinned. Hence, they are seeking a state of grace in this life in which their emotions and desires will never be stirred or enticed by a forbidden object. They might as well seek a state of animal life in which the heart will cease to throb and the machinery of life continue to move. This is the class of errorists who cry aloud for a complete self-crucifixion—such a crucifixion as would *destroy* instead of *regulate* and *control* all the lower affinities of our twofold nature. This is the error which has produced nearly all the fanatics who have bewildered one-half of the Church on the subject of sanctification, and disgusted the other half by their wild vagaries; and this is the error that built all the monasteries and nunneries of the Dark Ages, and which has led thousands to self-contempt—a crime as pernicious as pride!

"But, is there no state of grace in

this life in which we are saved from evil desires?" Yes; but no desire can be evil or become a lust without the sympathy and concurrence of the will. Up to the point where a man is "drawn away of his own desire and enticed" the solicitation is a temptation; but temptation resisted and foiled is neither an evil nor a sin. We cannot conceive how any being can sin except as a moral agent, and we cannot see how a moral agent can sin aside from volition.

Again, we may reach the will from the opposite direction—from within—by another road. We said that there is another class of emotions belonging to the mind, called the moral emotions. These are followed by feelings of moral obligation. Desires are founded on the natural emotions, while the obligatory feelings are based exclusively on the moral emotions. But the desires agree with the obligatory feelings in being in direct contact with the volitive power; so that the will, in making up its final decision, takes immediate notice of only the desires, on the one hand, and the interdictions of the obligatory feelings on the other; and in every temptation these two classes of mental states stand before the will in direct and fierce opposition to each other. In the cravings of desire and the interdictions of obligation we have the basis of an internal conflict that may be renewed every day and every hour. These two opposing principles were shut up together in our twofold nature as it came from the hand of its Creator, and they are destined to renew the conflict with every new temptation during life. To try to escape it is to try to put ourselves beyond the sphere of temptation and to close up our state of probation.

As we shall show farther on, not a few mental states, which have been called the "remains of the carnal mind," "inbred sin," and "sin in believers," are nothing more than the *consciousness* of this internal conflict which always accompanies a severe temptation, but is more keenly felt in the early part of the Christian life on account of the force of old habits. The idea that religion, at regeneration or afterward, does something for us that so destroys our natural sensibilities as to make them no longer susceptible of being "enticed" by evil, has been the source of untold agony among those who have tried to reach such a state. I have known more than one mind dethroned by a failure to reach this impossible state.

It is time that the Christian world, and especially all Christian teachers, were learning that whatever grace does for us is done according to the fixed laws of the mind, and not by setting these laws aside or by destroying any part of our twofold nature. For the want of recognizing this fact many have been led to believe that they had the "former corruption of the heart remaining in them and striving for the mastery," when in reality they had only "suffered, being tempted," as did their divine Master before them. The remedy in all such cases is not to be found in the conclusion that sin is unavoidable, nor in the idea that regeneration is a "*partial* renovation," leaving a "residue of sin within us," but in rejecting the temptation. These sensibilities, through which the temptation makes its approach, belong to and are inseparable from the constitution of man. The fact that we are commanded to "make no provision for the flesh, to fulfill the desires thereof," is proof positive that the flesh is not to be so crucified as to destroy its susceptibility of being "enticed;" for without that susceptibility we could not be tempted of evil. And the fact that we may be "tempted without sin" is proof that the stirrings of the emotions and the enkindlings of the desires, aside from the concurrence of the will, are not sinful; neither are they any proof that the "former corruptions of the heart remain in those who are regenerated."

Prof. B. B. Edwards says: "To say that all excitement of these susceptibilities is itself sin is to say that there is no difference between voluntary and involuntary desires; it is to say that sin is unavoidable. To admit, however, that the excitement of these susceptibilities is not in itself a sin and, unless they be indulged by the will, leaves the being as holy as ever, is merely to admit that there is such a thing possible as the temptation of a being who remains sinless."

St. James says: "Let no man say when he is tempted, I am tempted of God: for God cannot be tempted with evil, neither tempteth he any man: but every man is tempted, when he is drawn away of his own desire and enticed. Then when desire hath conceived it bringeth forth sin." (James i. 13, 14, 15.) In this delicate figure St. James represents desire, even under enticement, as preserving virgin purity until defiled by volition.

We now have the key to unlock the mysteries of the most obscure and difficult passages in Mr. Wesley's works—especially that mysterious sermon on "Sin in Believers." But we must defer the investigation of that sermon until the next chapter. There are expressions in other books, which may be noticed now, which the authors would never have made if they had understood the twofold nature of man and the philosophy of temptation.

Dr. J. Dempster says: "Regeneration admits of controlled tendencies to sin; entire sanctification extirpates those tendencies."

Now these "controlled tendencies to sin" in a regenerated soul are nothing more than a consciousness of the natural "desires being drawn out and enticed," which, according to St. James, is the very essence of temptation. To "extirpate these tendencies" would simply destroy man's essential nature, and put him where he "could not be tempted of evil"—a perfection which belongs to God, and not to man.

Dr. D. Curry says: "This carnal mind survives the work of regeneration, and is often actively rebellious in the hearts of real Christians." The learned doctor would hardly have said that if he had taken off his theological spectacles when he read Paul on the "carnal mind" and the "spiritually minded," "the natural man" and "the spiritual man," "the old man" and "the new man." That "real Christians" often feel the uprisings of desire creating a fierce conflict within is very true; even the holy "Jesus suffered, being tempted." But no man was ever a "real Christian" and had the "carnal mind in his heart" at the same time. To say that the "carnal mind survives the work of regeneration" is to say that a regenerated man is not reconciled to God, "because the carnal mind is enmity against God;" and wherever it exists it exists in a state of "active rebellion," for "it is not *subject* to the *law of God*, neither indeed can be." Hence, regeneration either "destroys the body of sin"—"the carnal mind"—or else it fails to reconcile us to God. This "carnal mind" is the "law of sin and death that reigns in the unregenerate," and from which, Paul affirms, "the law of the Spirit of life in Christ Jesus makes us *free;*" and "if the Son make you free, you shall be *free indeed:*" but "if any man have not this Spirit of life in Christ Jesus, he is none of his." If Paul had written the sixth and eighth chapters of Romans to overthrow the "residue theory of regeneration," he could not have made his arguments stronger or his points clearer.

Dr. Luther Lee says: "There is still a warfare within; there will be found an opposing element in the sensibilities of the soul, which, though it no longer controls the will, often rebels against it and refuses to obey it. . . . This must be brought into harmony with the sanctified will before the whole soul can be said to be sanctified. When this work is wrought, then the war within will cease."

Now the Doctor's "warfare within"—his "opposing element in the sensibility of the soul"—is the very essence of temptation, and is realized to a greater or less degree in every solicitation to evil; it was thus that "Christ suffered, being tempted." Hence, to destroy this "sensibility of the soul," so that the "war within will cease," is to put us beyond the susceptibility of being tempted. Hence, Dr. Knapp truly says: "The desires of man are not in themselves and abstractly considered sinful, for they are deep laid in the constitution which God has given to human nature; and they arise in man involuntarily, and so far cannot be imputed to him." And Prof. Stuart goes farther and says: "With the deepest reverence I say it: The Lord Jesus Christ himself had a *susceptibility of feeling the power of enticement to sin*, like that which Adam had before the fall. If not, then he did not really and truly take on him *human nature.* The fact that such a state of susceptibility belonged to Adam in his primitive state shows that it belongs to human nature in its *perfect probationary state.*" ("Bib. Repos.," 1839.) Another able divine has said: "It was in this way that the temptation of Christ caused suffering; he suffered from the *force of desire.* Though there was no hesitation whether to obey or not, no strife in the will, yet in the act of mastery there was pain. There was *self-denial;* there was obedience at the expense of *tortured natural feeling;* 'Jesus suffered, being tempted.' He 'was tempted *like as we are;*' remember this, for the way in which some speak of the sinlessness of Jesus reduces all his suffering to physical pain, destroys the reality of temptation, reduces that glorious heart to a pretense, and converts the whole of his history into a mere fictitious drama, in which scenes of trial were represented, not felt!"

Once more: Rev. Wm. Bramwell, in a letter to a friend, says: "An idea is going forth that when we are justified, we are entirely sanctified, and that to feel evil nature after justification is to lose pardon. You may depend upon it, this is the devil's great gun. We shall have much trouble with this, and I am afraid we cannot suppress it."

The above paragraph is a remarkable utterance in itself; but to see the use that certain writers have made of it is still more remarkable. Now the phrase, "to feel evil nature after justification is to lose pardon," is exceedingly *equivocal*. If he means by "feeling evil nature" that the justified believer's nature has become evil by voluntary yielding to temptation, then there can be no controversy about "pardon being lost." But if he means by "feeling evil nature" the susceptibility of feeling enticement to sin, then, so far from that forfeiting pardon, no state of grace in this life will free us from that susceptibility. So the *"devil's great gun"* is spiked by drawing the line between temptation and sin—between the susceptibility to feel enticement to evil and the will yielding to the solicitation. From the above extract from Mr. Bramwell's letters, and one or two remarks of Mr. Wesley, we believe if those who contended in that day that regeneration and sanctification are coetaneous had drawn the line between temptation and sin—had drawn it clearly and sharply—then the "residue theory" would never have been so generally received. The truth is, both schools of theologians of that day frequently confounded temptation and sin. The one class called it "inbred sin," the "remains of the carnal mind," which, said they, does not forfeit pardon, but makes a "second change necessary." The other class contended that sin was sin, and that where sin actually existed pardon was forfeited. They were both right and both wrong. Every sin after justification forfeits pardon, but temptation is not sin. There are thousands of cases where not only a "second cleansing" is necessary, but a third, a fourth, and, in some cases, one hundred "cleansings" and "blessings" will be received during life; but in all such cases the "foundation for repentance" and a "second cleansing" originated "from dead works" and "defiled garments," and the loss of their "first love," and not because "regeneration is a partial renovation"—all of which will be made clear as we advance in this investigation. But having captured and spiked the "*devil's great gun,*" we will stop and rest, and renew the battle in the next chapter.

CHAPTER III.
"Sin in Believers."

OUR respect for Mr. Wesley is profound. He did more than any other one man to clear up the muddy theology of the Dark Ages. If he failed to harmonize his theory of the divine life at some points, he did more than any other man of modern times—Luther not excepted—to quicken that life in the souls of men. When he "saw, from reading the Bible, that he could not be saved without holiness," if he had expurgated the "residue theory of regeneration" from *his* Creed, as he finally expurgated it from the Creed he prepared for the Methodist Church of America, his body of divinity would have been the most harmonious and Biblical ever given to the world. But that "dead fly in his pot of precious ointment" has been the source of confusion in doctrine and experience through all the history of Methodism. None but those who have read his "Journals" for that express purpose have any correct idea of the amount of trouble and confusion this "residue theory" brought upon Mr. Wesley. A few, and only a few, know something of the magnitude of the trouble and confusion it has introduced into the theology and experience of American Methodism; and we fear the end is not yet.

As much as Mr. Wesley wrote, he never wrote any thing so at war with the fundamental principles of the divine life, as taught and explained by himself and set forth in the Word of God, as what he wrote in defense of "Sin in

Believers." Starting from the standpoint of the Ninth Article of the Church of England, instead of the Bible, he failed to see that all the mental states he describes, as well as the Scripture texts he quotes, can be accounted for and explained without adopting the "residue theory." No one can carefully read the first part of the sermon on "Sin in Believers" without being impressed with the fact that Mr. Wesley, more under the influence of the "remains of High-churchism" than under a consciousness of the "remains of the carnal mind," regarded the "residue theory" as being *settled by Church authority;* and, as a loyal son of the Church, he went to work to defend this dogma (against the teachings of Count Zinzendorf) by appealing to the canons of the Church, the Fathers, and such Scripture texts as might bear such application. If any thing had quietly led him to suspect that a great error was couched in this dogma of the Church he would have rejected it, as he did the dogmas of "apostolic succession" and "baptismal regeneration." We are confirmed in this opinion by the fact that Mr. Wesley did finally *reject this dogma so far as to cut it out of the Articles of Faith prepared for the Church to be organized in America!*

But to return: While Mr. Wesley was intensely engaged in *reviving* primitive Christianity as a living power in the soul—preaching holiness of heart and life everywhere he went—Messrs. Bell, Maxfield, and others in the Society in London came forward and testified that they had found this Bible holiness, having received "sanctification" as a "second change." As this opened the way to reach the great object for which he groaned (Bible holiness), without colliding with the Ninth Article of the Church, Mr. Wesley accepted the testimony of these witnesses on the one hand, and the "residue" dogma of the Church on the other hand, and thus he was committed to the "residue theory of regeneration" and the "second change theory of sanctification;" and his sermons on "Sin in Believers" and "The Repentance of Believers" were an earnest effort of a great mind and a ripe scholar to harmonize these two theories with Christian experience and the teaching of the Bible. But he *failed;* and if John Wesley failed, there must be a great error hid away in one or both of these "theories."

To see such a man as Mr. Wesley—

learned, clear, and logical on all other subjects—struggling, floundering, first on this side, now on that side of his subject, is one of the saddest scenes in the life of that great man. Have I made it too strong? Let us see. On this side he says: "We allow that the state of a justified person is inexpressibly great and glorious. . . . He is created anew in Christ Jesus; he is washed; he is *sanctified.* His heart is *purified* by faith; he is *cleansed* from the corruption that is in the world." "To be born again is to be *inwardly* changed from *all sinfulness to all holiness.*" Now on the other side he says: "If there be no such *second change after justification,* . . . then we must be content, as well as we can, to remain *full of sin till death;* and, if so, we must remain *guilty till death,* continually deserving punishment." Now, I submit that any "theory" of the divine life that involved such a man as Mr. Wesley in such absurdities and self-contradictions as the above must be at war with reason, common sense, and the Word of God!

There is much in the writings of Wesley, Fletcher, Clarke, and Watson which will quadrate with the Ninth Article of the Church of England, from which stand-point they all wrote; but I thank God from the depths of my soul that this "residue" dogma was never in the Articles of Faith of either branch of the Methodist Episcopal Church in America. "But it is in our standard works on theology." True; and it is in a great many more that are not "standard works;" but it is equally true that all these "standard authors," in defining the new birth, have admitted and affirmed every thing we contend for in regeneration. Hence, we not only have our Articles of Faith on our side, but, if the language of the Fathers—the authority of the "standards"—is worth any thing, it is worth as much to us as to those who hold to the "residue theory." When doctors and masters differ the pupils can take either side. If Mr. Wesley and the other Fathers of Methodism adopted a "theory" which they could not harmonize with itself, nor reconcile with the plain teaching of the Word of God, nor with their own expositions of that Word—expositions given by them when they were searching for the mind of the Spirit, as expressed in the language of the text in the light of the context—shall we adopt the said "*theory*," or decide with the Bible and the *unbiased* expositions of the Bible given by these aforesaid Fathers? One had about as well go to our Articles of Faith, after Mr. Wesley completed his work of expurgation, to find the "residue theory," as to search for it in Clarke's "Commentary" and Wesley's "Notes on the New Testament." Mr. Wesley's sermons on "Sin in Believers" and the "Repentance of Believers" were both written and published under peculiar circumstances, to meet the follies and excesses of Bell, Maxfield, and their followers. Dr. J. T. Crane, who has looked up all the facts and dates, says: "Bell and the other enthusiasts professed to have become so holy that they were out of the reach of temptation, and denounced all who failed to attain the same fancied heights. Not content with a 'second' work of grace, by which, as they claimed, their hearts were wholly purified from evil tempers, they began to profess a '*third*,' by which their minds, as they said, were lifted above the reach of evil thoughts. Wesley's sermon on 'Sin in Believers' was designed to be a refutation of these unscriptural notions." Yet, in reading the books and periodicals published in this country in the interest of the "residue theory," one would almost be led to conclude that when "our standards" are referred to, one or the other of these sermons is the document intended. Such importance being given to these two sermons, it becomes necessary in this investigation to give them a thorough examination. But before I begin this analysis let me call attention to two significant historical facts. First, in 1784, only seven years before his death, Mr. Wesley rejected the "residue theory" so far as to cut it out of our Articles of Faith. Second, in 1785, one year later, he published his sermon on "Perfection," in which he says not a word about "inbred sin" or "the seeds of sin in believers." Add a third fact: In 1763, over twenty-eight years before his death, he published his sermon on "Sin in Believers," under the peculiar circumstances already described. I leave these facts with the reader for the present.

I have selected four paragraphs from the two sermons referred to; and as these paragraphs have been transcribed into all the books and periodicals printed in the interest of the "residue theory of regeneration" and the "second change theory of sanctification;" and as these paragraphs state these two theories as strongly as language can—

being the key-note of all the modern writers of this school—I hope their selection will be satisfactory. After we have examined them in the light of the facts brought out in the last chapter, we will examine proof-texts.

Mr. Wesley says: (1) "That [justified] believers are delivered from the *guilt* and *power* of sin we allow; that they are delivered from its *being* we deny." (2) "Christ indeed cannot reign where sin *reigns;* neither will he dwell where any sin is allowed. But he is and dwells in the heart of every believer who is fighting against all sin, although the heart be not yet purified." (Ser. XIII.)

What Mr. Wesley means by the "*being* of sin" and a "heart not yet *purified*" is the "*infection* of our nature," which the Ninth Article says "remains in them that are regenerated. . . . And although there is no condemnation for them that believe, yet this *corruption* hath of itself the *nature of sin.*" Hence, Mr. Wesley calls it "inbred sin," indwelling sin," the "being of sin." Paul calls it "the old man," "body of sin," "sin that dwelleth in" the "carnal" or "natural man," "the law of sin which was in my members," when he "was carnal, sold under sin," "the law of sin and death," and "the carnal mind." Now the difference between Paul and the Ninth Article of the Church of England is that Paul used every one of these terms to describe the condition of the *unregenerated* man, while the Ninth Article applies them to the *regenerated believer;* and Mr. Wesley, like a loyal Churchman, followed the Article of Faith instead of Paul! And hundreds in this country have followed Mr. Wesley! The difference between St. Paul and Mr. Wesley is that Paul says that "the old man is crucified," the "body of sin is destroyed," and that we are "made free from the law of sin and death," when we "put off the old man and put on the new man, which, according to the divine pattern, is created in righteousness and true holiness;" while Mr. Wesley says that "if there be no *second change after justification, then we must remain full of sin until death!*" In the sixth chapter of Romans Paul teaches clearly that the *normal* state of the divine life in the soul includes or presupposes a "crucifixion of the old man," a "destruction of the body of sin," and a "death to sin." This is so clearly his meaning that Dr. A. Clarke says: "The man who has received

Christ Jesus by faith and has been made a partaker of the Holy Spirit has had his old man destroyed, so that he is not only justified freely from all sin, but WHOLLY *sanctified!*" In Romans viii. 1-4 Paul, in describing the results of justifying faith, says: "The law of the spirit of life in Christ Jesus hath made me free from the law of sin and death." It is so clear that Paul here teaches that justification is immediately followed by *entire* sanctification that Dr. Clarke says: "The gospel *pardons* and *sanctifies;* the *carnal man,* laboring under the overpowering influence of the sin of his nature, . . . is first freely justified—he feels no condemnation; he is FULLY *sanctified*—he walks not after the *flesh,* but after the *spirit.*"

Again Mr. Wesley says: (3) "Indeed, this grand point that there are two contrary principles in believers—nature and grace, the flesh and spirit—runs through all the Epistles of St. Paul—yea, through all the Holy Scriptures: almost all the directions and exhortations therein are founded on this supposition, pointing at wrong tempers or practices in those who are, notwithstanding, acknowledged by the inspired writers to be believers." (Ser. XIII.)

The first point we notice in this paragraph is: the facts do not sustain the inferences. The fact that "there are two contrary principles in believers—nature and grace, the flesh and spirit"—does not sustain the inference that there is "sin in believers;" for Christ had "nature and grace, the flesh and spirit" in him, or else he was not truly a man. The fact that the gospel proposes to "destroy the *body of sin*," to "crucify the *old man*," (which is inbred sin itself) does not sustain the inference that one of our two natures must be destroyed. Any one can see that the work proposed in this "second change" is to destroy "nature" and leave "grace," to destroy the "flesh" and leave the "spirit;" to deny this would be to make Mr. Wesley write nonsense!

Of course "almost all the directions and exhortations in Holy Scripture are founded upon the supposition that nature and grace, the flesh and spirit are in believers;" for if regeneration, or sanctification either, "destroyed the nature or flesh of a believer," then there would be no need of either "directions or exhortations," for said believer would then be no longer exposed to the temptation of "making provision for the flesh," or any other temptation. But to say that "Christ will dwell in a heart not yet purified," and that those who are "indulging wrong *tempers* and *practices* are nevertheless justified believers"—to say all this, and more, in order to make occasion for a "second change," is to put the "residue theory of regeneration" and the "second change theory of sanctification" on a sandy foundation indeed!

Once more. Mr. Wesley says: (4) "By all the grace given at justification, though we watch and pray ever so much, we cannot wholly cleanse either our hands or our hearts. Most sure we cannot, till it please our Lord to speak to our hearts *again*, to speak the *second time*, 'Be clean!' and then only the leprosy is cleansed; then only the evil root, the *carnal mind*, is destroyed, and *inbred sin* subsists no more. But if there be no such *second change after justification,* . . . then we must be content, as well as we can, to remain *full of sin till death;* and, if so, we must remain *guilty till death, continually deserving punishment!*" (Ser. XIV.)

This is a remarkable paragraph in many respects, but mainly in that it is the only place in which Mr. Wesley admits that "Sin in Believers" involves "*guilt*" and "deserves *punishment!*" How a man can be "*full of sin and guilt, so as to deserve punishment*" and be in a "*justified state*" at the same time, is beyond my comprehension. And yet to say that such a man has forfeited his justification and needs this second change to re-instate him is to give up the "residue theory of regeneration" and the "second change theory of sanctification!" Of these alternatives I have chosen the latter. But a state of *guilt* and *justification* can be reconciled about as easily as to conceive how the "*carnal mind*" can exist in a regenerated believer and remain there "till it please the Lord to speak *again*, to speak the *second* time, 'Be clean!'"* Will the Christian world never learn that the mind God gave to man in creation is the same mind that he carries with him forever? and that the "*carnal mind*" is nothing more than this same mind under the control of our fleshly nature—"the course of carnal thinking?" and that all that is necessary to "destroy the carnal mind" is to "renew us in the divine image" and take this same mind from under the control of this fleshly

---

* We have already shown that regeneration either destroys the "carnal mind," or else it fails to reconcile us to God.

nature and put it back under the control of the Holy Spirit and our renewed spiritual nature, so that we will "walk not after the flesh but after the Spirit?" And will learned theologians never learn that in this work of "transforming and renewing the mind," neither one of our two natures is destroyed? that the "old man," the "body of sin," "inbred sin," and the "carnal mind," all mean the same thing in Paul's psychology? and that the "old man is crucified," the "body of sin is destroyed," the "carnal mind is destroyed," and "inbred sin subsists no more" when we "put off the old man, and put on the new man?"

How any man who has studied Paul's Epistle to the Romans can talk about "destroying the carnal mind in a regenerated believer," who has not forfeited his justified state by "walking after the flesh," is a mystery I cannot understand; for no one can be "born of the Spirit" without becoming "spiritually minded," and Paul shows conclusively that no one can be "carnally minded" and "spiritually minded" at the same time. There is no half-way house on this "Appian Way" to the spiritual kingdom. Even Mr. Wesley has said: "That which is born of the Spirit is *spiritual, heavenly, divine, like its Author.*" "To be born again is to be *inwardly changed from all sinfulness to all holiness.*" This point cannot be evaded by using the term, "the remains of the carnal mind," for there is nothing to remain." Man has but one mind, and that mind is either carnal or spiritual, according as he "walks after the flesh" or "after the Spirit." If a man can walk in opposite directions at the same time, then he can be "carnally minded" and "spiritually minded"— then he can be a "justified believer" and be "full of sin and guilt" at the same time; but not till then.

Paul's argument runs thus: There can be no carnal mind in those who walk not after the flesh, but after the Spirit; for they that walk after the flesh do mind the things of the flesh; but they that walk after the Spirit do mind the things of the Spirit. For to be carnally minded is spiritual death; but to be spiritually minded is life and peace. Because the carnal mind is enmity against God: for it is not subject to the law of God, neither indeed can be. So then, they that walk after the flesh cannot please God. But ye walk not after the flesh, but after the Spirit, *if so be the Spirit of God dwell in you. Now if any man have not the Spirit of Christ dwelling in him,* HE IS NONE OF HIS.* Hence, so long as the Spirit dwells in the heart of a believer, and he "makes no provision for the flesh to fulfill the desires thereof," so long there will be no "carnal mind" in him to be destroyed; and hence no need of this "second change."

Again, if there be "sin in justified believers," and if "we cannot wholly cleanse our hearts, till it please the Lord to speak to our hearts again, to speak the second time, 'Be clean!'" does it not follow that this "sin" is allowed to "remain in our hearts" under the *divine approval*? The truth is, ac-

---

* In the above paraphrase of Rom. viii. 4–9 I have given a clearer idea of Paul's argument than can be given by the ordinary mode of comment.

cording to the whole statement of the case by Mr. Wesley, this "residue theory" charges God with the folly of *forgiving sin*, the "being and corruption" of which he allows to "*remain* till he speaks to our hearts again, till he speaks the second time, 'Be clean!'" We ask, in the name of Christianity, is this the best the gospel can do for fallen, depraved, corrupt humanity? Let St. John answer: "If we confess our sins, he is faithful and just to forgive us our sins and to cleanse us from *all unrighteousness*." Yea, let Mr. Wesley himself answer: "To be born again is to be *inwardly changed from all sinfulness to all holiness*." When defining the new birth Mr. Wesley always gave a Bible definition of regeneration, but when he came to speak of sanctification as a "second change" he always became entangled and collided with himself. This theory of the divine life never has been harmonized with itself or reconciled with the plain teaching of the Word of God. We believe, and have undertaken to show, that the "residue theory of regeneration" and the "second change theory of sanctification" rest upon a false psychology and a misapplication of a few texts of Scripture. Mr. Wesley was led into the one by the Ninth Article of the Church of England, and he accepted the other upon the testimony of some of the members of his society in London. But "Mr. Wesley had scarcely left London, after receiving this testimony, before two of these witnesses, George Bell and Thomas Maxfield, began to hold independent meetings, declaring that no one could teach the sanctified except those who were themselves in that state of grace; and that God was to be found only among these his saints."* "These enthusiasts professed to have become so holy that they were out of the reach of temptation,† and denounced all who failed to

---

*"Maxfield carried off finally about two hundred members, founded an independent congregation, and continued to minister to them for twenty years, and then died. Bell turned prophet, and declared that the world would come to an end on the 28th of February, 1763. When his prophecy was proved false by time, he not only gave up the office of prophet, but abandoned all pretense of religion, went into politics, and died an infidel." Will not our members who are being led out of the Methodist Church by self-appointed teachers take warning? And will not the leaders of these "Holiness Conventions" pause and "*go slow?*" There may be danger ahead, around the curve!

† This was a natural result of the "residue theory." Having mistaken the essence of temptation for the "motions of inbred sin," the "remains of

attain the same fancied heights." Thus the " residue theory " gave Mr. Wesley trouble as long as he lived, and among the great and latest acts of his wonderful life, he cut out that clause of the Ninth Article which taught it, and gave American Methodists a Creed from which this Antinomian error was expurgated. We are now ready to examine proof-texts.

the carnal mind," and their " second change" (designed to remove this) failing to relieve them, then they were ready for any delusion that might suggest itself.

CHAPTER IV.

"How Readest Thou?"

WHILE every Christian feels that his experience agrees, in the main, with those mental states which Mr. Wesley describes in his sermon on "Sin in Believers," yet all those mental states can be accounted for without adopting the "residue theory of regeneration." We believe that every text quoted and every mental state described readily and naturally resolve themselves into one of two classes: First, the parties referred to were persons who were passing through severe temptations, out of which they came as pure as ever; or, second, persons who had yielded to temptation in some form, and thereby forfeited their justification and "defiled their garments." To come directly to the point: If there be any force in habit, if passions and desires become strong by exercise and undue indulgence, if the young Christian be subjected to temptation, it follows that he will be severely exercised by the uprising of his desires at the presentation of a once enjoyed but now renounced object. But to say that so long as the will rejects the temptation there is sin is to say that temptation is sin; and if the will yields to say that such a one is still in a justified state is to say that voluntary transgression does not forfeit justification. Thus we shall find that the mental states which have been described as "sin in believers," and as being "compatible with a state of justification," are, in many instances, nothing more than severe temptations, and as such were not sinful; in other cases, however, it is equally clear that the will had concurred with the solicitation, and justification was forfeited.

Mr. Wesley himself says: "The more any believer examines his own heart the more will he be convinced of this—that faith, working by love, excludes both inward and outward sin from the soul watching unto prayer; that, nevertheless, we are liable, even then, to be tempted, particularly to the sin that did so easily beset us; that if the loving eye of the soul be steadfastly fixed on God the temptation soon vanishes away; but if not—if we are 'drawn out by our own desires,' and *caught* by the bait of present or promised pleasure, then that desire conceived in us [indulged] brings forth sin." What a pity that a man who had such clear views of the Bible idea of the new birth and temptation as Mr. Wesley should have been tied hand and foot by a Church dogma so at war with both. No wonder he drew his pen through that *clause* in preparing our Articles of Faith.

But we promised to explain the proof-texts. "What is written in the law? How readest thou?" Let us begin with 1 Cor. iii. 1, 2, 3. In the preceding chapter Paul draws a clear distinction between the natural man and the new man, or the carnal man and the spiritual man; and then begins this chapter thus: "And I, brethren, could not speak unto you as spiritual [men], but as unto carnal [men]; . . . for whereas there are among you envying, and strife, and divisions, are ye not carnal, and walk as [carnal] men?" (1

Cor. iii. 1, 2, 3.) Dr. Clarke says:' "Ye act just as the people of the world, and have no more of the spirit of religion than they. . . . These people were wrong in thought, word, and deed!" The fact that Paul speaks unto them, or had spoken unto them, "as babes in Christ," and "fed them with milk, and not with meat, because they were not able to bear it," does not prove that these "carnal men" were then in a justified state; for the context shows that the state of babyhood refers to *knowledge* instead of *moral condition* (See Dr. Clarke *in loco*). Moreover, Paul says positively that he "could not speak unto them as unto *spiritual* men"— "Now if any man have not the Spirit of Christ, he is none of his;" but Paul could and did "speak unto them as unto *carnal men*"—and "to be carnally minded is [spiritual] death." Does not that settle the question that these "carnal men," or, if you prefer, these "natural men" were in a state of spiritual death and condemnation? Again, Paul said that they "walked as [carnal] men;" and "they that walk after the flesh cannot please God." Once more: if these "carnal men" were still in a *justified* state, they were also in a *sanctified* state; for Paul, in addressing this Church, says: "Unto the Church of God which is at Corinth, to them that are *sanctified* in Christ Jesus," etc.; "ye are washed, ye are sanctified, ye are justified in the name of the Lord Jesus, and by the Spirit of God." (1 Cor. i. 2; vi. 11.) So those "*carnal* men" had either forfeited their justified state, or else a degree of *carnality* is also left in a *sanctified* believer! In either case the text (1 Cor. iii. 1, 2, 3) proves nothing for the "residue theory of regeneration" and the "second change theory of sanctification."

The next proof-text is Gal. v. 17: "For the flesh lusteth against the Spirit, and the Spirit lusteth against the flesh." Now every thing affirmed of the flesh is affirmed of the Holy Spirit in this verse; hence the word "lust" is a mistranslation in both the sixteenth and seventeenth verses. The whole chapter shows conclusively that so far from Paul intending to teach in this text (verse 17) that moral "corruption," or the "carnal mind," could abide in a regenerated believer so as to really "lust" after a forbidden object, he intended to teach that a "carnal" and a "spiritual" life were so diametrically opposed that we could not commingle the two, but we passed immediately from the one state to the other as soon as we tried to combine them in the same heart. After telling some of these Galatians that they had "fallen from grace" (verse 4), Paul goes on to say: "Walk in the Spirit, and ye shall not fulfill the desires of the flesh. For the flesh desireth against the Spirit, and the Spirit desireth against the flesh, (and these are contrary the one to the other) that ye may not do the things ye would. But if ye are led by the Spirit ye are not under the [condemnation] of the law." (Mr. Wesley's trans. Gal. v. 16, 17, 18.) So far, then, from these Galatians who were "fulfilling the desires of the flesh" being in a justified state and a sample of all justified believers, they refused to "walk in the Spirit," or to be "led by the Spirit," and were "under the [condemnation] of the law." Dr. Clarke says: "They had fallen from the grace of the gospel; and as Christ no longer dwelt in their hearts by faith, pride, anger, ill-will, and all unkind and uncharitable tempers took possession of their souls; and they were, in consequence, alternately destroying each other. . . . It was on this ground that Paul exhorted them to walk in the Spirit, that they might not fulfill the desires of the flesh; as without the grace of God they could do nothing." On the seventeenth verse Dr. Clarke remarks: "God still continues to strive with you, notwithstanding your *apostasy*, showing you whence you are fallen, and exciting you to return to him; but your own obstinacy renders all ineffectual, and through the influence of these different principles [the desires of the flesh and the convictions of the Spirit] you are kept in a state of self-opposition and self-distraction, 'so that ye cannot do the things that ye would.'" So far, then, from Gal. v. 17 teaching that a regenerated man may have "inbred sin," the "carnal mind," and "lust" abiding in him, we find that the persons referred to in that text were "*fulfilling* the desires of the flesh;" having ceased "to walk in the Spirit," or to be "led by the Spirit," they had forfeited their justification, had "fallen from grace," and were "under the [condemnation of the] law!"

We notice next 1 Thess. v. 23: "And the very God of peace sanctify you wholly; and I pray God your whole spirit and soul and body be preserved blameless unto the coming of our Lord Jesus Christ." Now, the *sum total* of which Paul speaks is the *whole man*, and not of a *partial* cleansing of the moral nature at one time and a complete cleansing of the moral nature at a subsequent time. It is one thing to be "pure in heart," and another thing to preserve a pure heart by a holy or pure life; and as Paul had exhorted them to "be at peace among themselves," to "warn the unruly," to "see that none render evil for evil," to "pray without ceasing," to "quench not the Spirit," to "abstain from all appearance of evil;" and then prayed that they might be "sanctified *wholly*" (not *holy*), and that their "spirit and soul and body might be preserved blameless," it is clear that he had his eye on such a "*consecration*" of the *whole man* as would lead to a "*blameless*" life, and that such an idea as the "residue theory" and the "second change theory" never entered Paul's mind.

The prayer of David is introduced as proof of the "residue theory:" "Create in me a clean heart, O God; and renew a right spirit within me." (Ps. li. 10.) But the necessity of a "clean heart" in this case did not originate in a "*partial renovation*" at conversion, but in the fact that David had committed a heinous sin after his feet had been taken out of the mire and clay, and a "new song put in his mouth;" hence he prayed also that a right spirit might be "renewed in him."

We pause here to call attention to a psychological fact that will give us the key of interpretation to those passages yet to be examined. We refer to the fact that in all such mental and spiritual activity as is put forth in the act of giving up the world and accepting Christ, there is produced in our mental nature what mental philosophers call a *"radical disposition."* * This "disposition" is usually referred to, in Christian experience, as "my original purpose to serve God and get to heaven." Now, as this "purpose" *precedes* regeneration, and is distinct from the spiritual life in the soul, it follows that a man may retain this purpose after he has forfeited his justified state and become spiritually dead. Thus it was with the Churches at Pergamos, Ephesus, Sardis, etc. None of these Churches had "denied the faith," none had renounced Christianity, none had given up their "original purpose to serve God and get to heaven;" yet in some of

---

* See Dr. Hickok's "Science of the Mind," page 335.

them even this "thing which remained was ready to die," and in all these Churches, except one, there was some open violation of God's laws which involved the guilty parties in condemnation, and for which they were commanded to "repent and do their first works." (See Rev. ii., iii.) Now these cases are held up to prove that regeneration is a *partial* work, leaving a residue of "corruption in them that are regenerated." In his sermon on "Sin in Believers" Mr. Wesley labors hard to show that all these backslidden members in these Churches were still in a justified state and fair representatives of all believers who had not received a "second change." But Christ said to them at Ephesus: "Thou hast left thy first love. Remember, therefore, from whence *thou art fallen, and repent, and do thy first works.*" (Rev. ii. 4, 5.) To them at Pergamos Christ said: "**Thou hast them that hold the doctrine of Balaam, who taught Balak to cast a stumbling-block before the children of Israel, to eat things sacrificed unto idols, and to commit fornication. So hast thou also them that hold the doctrine of the Nicolaitans,** *which thing I hate.** *Repent;* or else I will come unto thee quickly, and will fight against them with the sword of my mouth." (Rev. ii. 14, 15, 16.)

---

* Such were Mr. Wesley's "New Testament justified believers" when he was trying to prove the "residue dogma of the Church." Yet he wrote thus to Dr. Clarke: "If you can prove that any of our preachers or leaders, either directly or *indirectly*, speak against perfect love let him be a preacher or a leader no longer. I doubt whether he should continue in the Society. Because he that could speak thus in our congregation *cannot be an honest man.*" So much for a "theory."

To them at Sardis Christ said: "I know thy works, that thou hast a name, that thou livest, and *art dead.*" (Rev. iii. 7.) Comment is unnecessary. But in commenting on these three Churches Mr. Wesley failed to tell us that the remedy which Christ prescribed for these evils was to "*repent and do thy first* works;" while he prescribed a "second change;" that Christ charged their condition to wrong doing and thinking, while he accounted for it upon the supposition that "regeneration is a partial cleansing," leaving a "residue of corruption in them that are regenerated." Mr. Wesley also failed to tell us that Christ said of the Church at Sardis: "Thou hast a few names even in Sardis which have *not defiled their garments;* and they shall walk with me in white: for they are worthy." It is clear, then, that Mr.

Wesley's representative "justified believers" had all "*defiled their garments.*" And we believe as strongly as Mr. Wesley that all such need a "second cleansing;" and with the Master that all such should "repent and do their first works." But we must and do, in the fear of God, enter a solemn protest against the reason assigned by Mr. Wesley for this "repentance" and "second cleansing" as being repugnant to the Bible idea of regeneration and sanctification. If I were going to prove from the Bible that a justified believer can "fall from grace and forfeit his justified state," I would be willing to rest the whole case on the very texts and examples which Mr. Wesley has introduced to prove the "residue theory of regeneration." If any one will read and study every proof-text which has been quoted to sustain this "theory," in the light of Biblical psychology and a sound exegesis of the sacred text, all will be clear.

Our position, then, is this: Regeneration is a complete work and *includes* sanctification. Regeneration expresses the nature of the change and sanctification the result—*moral purity*. Then we draw a distinction between regeneration and Christian perfection. Regeneration is an *instantaneous* work resulting in moral purity, while perfection is a *growth* resulting in *maturity*. Let us examine this position in the light of Scripture. "How readest thou?"

The term "regeneration" is used only twice in the New Testament—once by Christ and once by Paul. As used by Christ (Matt. xix. 28) it refers to the "new order of things at the general resurrection." As used by Paul it refers to the work of grace in the heart which the Scriptures call sanctification. In proof of this we give the text, and then give Mr. Wesley's notes: "But after that the kindness and love of God our Saviour toward man appeared, not by works of righteousness which we have done, but according to his own mercy he saved us by the washing of regeneration and renewing of the Holy Ghost, which he poured forth richly upon us through Jesus Christ our Saviour, that being justified by his grace we might become heirs according to the hope of eternal life." (Titus iii. 4-7.)

Mr. Wesley says: "In this important passage the apostle presents us with a delightful view of our redemption. Herein we have, first, the cause of it: . . . second, the effects, which are,

(1) Justification—being justified, pardoned, and accepted through the alone merits of Christ. . . . (2) *Sanctification—expressed by the laver of regeneration and the renewal of the Holy Ghost, which purifies the soul and renews it in the whole image of God.*"

Observe, in the only place in the New Testament where regeneration is used to describe a work of grace in the heart it is used in the sense of *sanctification;* and in this place Paul puts it in direct connection with justification. In view of this fact, no wonder Mr. Watson says: "The regenerate state is also called in Scripture, sanctification." In the Bible sanctification means "to consecrate, to cleanse, to purify." Sanctification, then, is twofold; we must *consecrate* ourselves to God in order for him to cleanse or purify us from sin. Hence, "if we confess our sins he is faithful and just to forgive us our sins and to cleanse us from all unrighteousness;" for "the blood of Jesus Christ his Son cleanseth us from all sin." This all-cleansing blood is applied at "forgiveness" by the Holy Spirit as the agent, and by faith as the condition: "Being sanctified by the Holy Ghost;" "purifying their hearts by faith;" "ye are washed, ye are sanctified in the name of the Lord Jesus, and by the Spirit of God;" "that they may receive inheritance among them that are sanctified by faith." Now all this is precisely the same work of grace in the heart which Paul calls the "washing of regeneration and the renewing of the Holy Ghost"—"putting on the new man," "created anew in Christ Jesus," and the same as that which Christ calls "being born of the Spirit." These terms express the *nature* of regeneration, while sanctification expresses the *result*.

In the work of salvation the guilt of sin must be pardoned, the pollution of sin must be cleansed, man's spiritual nature must be "created anew," "born of the Spirit," "renewed in the image of God." Now all this is the work of God done for us and in us; it is all an instantaneous work, and in such *rapid* succession that it may be said it is all done *co-etaneously*. A partial creation, a partial new birth, a partial forgiveness is just as scriptural as a partial cleansing. Hence John declares in language that cannot be misunderstood: "If we confess our sins he is faithful and just to forgive us our sins, and to cleanse us from all unrighteousness;" and he pledges the justice and faithfulness of God to this divine *order* of things.

In referring to the Gentiles who were converted at the house of Cornelius, Peter says: "God put no difference between us and them, *purifying* their hearts by faith." Now if Peter had known that the "former corruptions of the heart remain in them that are regenerated," surely he would not have said "*purifying* their hearts," and affirmed the same of the "three thousand on the Day of Pentecost!" And if the apostles and elders to whom he was reporting had been a modern "Holiness Convention," I think some of them would have called him to order!

When the "Lord Jesus sent Paul to preach to the Gentiles," he sent him "to open their eyes, and to turn them from darkness to light, and from the power of Satan unto God, that they might receive *forgiveness* of sins, and inheritance among them that are *sanctified* by faith." (Acts xxv. 18.) Here, again, "forgiveness of sin" and "sanctification" are put in direct or immediate connection.

When Jesus speaks our sins forgiven he says: "Now are ye *clean* through the word which I have spoken unto you" (John xv. 3); or, "I will, Be thou *clean*," and the *work is done!* The "washing of regeneration" is not a "partial renovation," leaving the "former corruptions to remain in the heart;" for "he that is washed is *clean every whit.*" (John xiii. 10.) Mr. Wesley, then, had the highest authority for saying that the "washing of regeneration is sanctification."

Paul says: "Unto the Church of God

which is at Corinth, to them that are *sanctified* in Christ Jesus;" "ye are washed, ye are *sanctified*, ye are justified in the name of the Lord Jesus." (1 Cor. i. 2; vi. 11.) In both these passages Paul uses the term "sanctified" to describe the state of grace received at justification. So did the apostle Jude when he began his Epistle thus: "Jude, the servant of Jesus Christ, to them that are *sanctified* by God the Father, and *preserved* in Jesus Christ."

The idea suggested by every term used to express the work of regeneration indicates that the inspired writers regarded that work as being complete in *kind*, but not in *development*. The soul "forgiven and cleansed from all unrighteousness" is to reach maturity by "abiding in Christ" and "growing in grace," and not by a "second change," unless he has "left his first love" and "defiled his garments."

Those who hold that "sanctification is a second change to remove the corruption left in the heart at regeneration," have a great deal to say about "crucifying the flesh, the old man," and being "dead to sin." But unfortunately for their "theory," instead of this state of "crucifixion" and "death to sin" being a state of grace to be sought as a separate and distinct work *after* regeneration, Paul teaches clearly and pointedly that this state of "crucifixion and death to sin" is one of the marks of the new birth; and that there is no spiritual life unless it includes a death to sin and a life unto holiness. "They that *are* Christ's have *crucified* the flesh [the old man] with the affections and lusts" (Gal. v. 24), "that the *body* of sin might be *destroyed*" (Rom. vi. 6); and "being made *free from* [*inward and outward*]* *sin,* and become servants of God, ye have your fruit unto holiness" (Rom. vi. 22). Peter says: "See that ye love one another with a *pure heart fervently; being born again, not of corruptible seed, but incorruptible,* by the Word of God." "Christ bore our sins in his own body on the tree, that we, *being dead to sin,* should live unto righteousness." (1 Pet. i. 22, 23; ii. 24, 25.)

In the fifth and sixth chapter of Romans Paul discusses the effects of the fall, and then the nature, the condition, and the result of the new birth, or regeneration; and in the sixth chapter he

---

*To say that Paul does not include "inward" or "inbred sin" in this verse is to ignore the central thought in his argument. (See verse 6.)

makes a long, lucid argument to prove that the *normal* state of the "new man" includes, or presupposes, a "crucifixion of the old man," the "destruction of the body of sin," and a "death to sin;" for in Paul's Epistles "the old man" and "the new man" are opposite terms, and the two things they represent can no more dwell together than light and darkness, or life and death. In the seventh chapter he describes the condition of an *awakened* sinner as he struggles with the "old man," the "carnal mind," until he cries out, "O wretched man that I am! who shall deliver me from the *body* of this death?" (This "carnal mind," this "body of sin," this "old man," which I now see is a mass of moral corruption!) The deliverance comes "through Jesus Christ our Lord" (verse 25). Then the eighth chapter announces that "there is therefore now no condemnation to them which are in Christ Jesus; . . . for the law of the Spirit of life in Christ Jesus hath made me free from this law of sin and death," "*hath made me* FREE *from this* old man," "this body of sin," "this carnal mind," "this body of death," "this law of sin and death!!" Hence, so far from Paul teaching that the "corruption of our nature remains in them that are regenerated," he teaches that this "old man is crucified," and this "body of sin is destroyed," when we "put off the old man and put on the new man, which is created according to the divine pattern in uprightness and moral purity." (See the Greek text of Eph. iv. 24.)

Christ said: "That which is born of the flesh is flesh, and that which is born of the Spirit is spirit." (John iii. 6.) Dr.

Clarke says: "*Like* will beget *like*. The kingdom of God is spiritual and holy; and that which is born of the Spirit resembles the Spirit; for as he is who begat, so is he who is begotten of him. . . . This new birth implies the *renewing of the whole soul in righteousness and true holiness;* . . . *it comprehends not only pardon, but also sanctification or holiness.*" Mr. Wesley says: "That which is born of the Spirit is *spiritual, heavenly, divine, like its author.* . . . To be born again is to be *inwardly changed from all sinfulness to all holiness.*" Now it comes to this: As Methodists, we must either give up the doctrine of "*inherited depravity,*" or we must abandon the "residue theory of regeneration;" for if depraved "Adam begat a son in his own *likeness,* after his *image,*" then the soul that is "born of God," "of *incorruptible seed,*" " of the *Holy* Spirit," cannot be "*impure,*" cannot have "inbred sin remaining in it;" but it must be "*pure,*" "*cleansed from* ALL *unrighteousness,*" "*from* ALL *sin!*" How readest thou?

Dr. Clarke says: "The 'old man,' the 'body of sin' is the same which we mean by 'indwelling sin' or the 'infection of our nature,' in consequence of the fall." Now this depravity or "infection of our nature" creates the necessity of the new birth or regeneration;* but, strange to say, learned theologians (?) and Bishops (?) would have us believe, or stultify our common sense

---

*This is specially true of infants; for " our best authors hold that infants are born in a justified state, but need regeneration to cleanse the 'corruption naturally engendered of the offspring of Adam.'"

by trying to believe, that this "corruption of our nature remains in them that are regenerated!" Yea, the Church of England has baptized this error into her Creed and made it a part of her Ninth Article of Faith! Hence, the Church of England is consistent with herself and her Ninth Article when she holds and teaches "baptismal regeneration, and the eternal damnation of all infants dying unbaptized!" From such an error John Wesley saved American Methodism when he gave us an abridgment of the Thirty-nine Articles of the Church of England. But is it not time for our General Conference to appoint a committee to *expunge* this "*residue theory*" from our standard works, as Mr. Wesley *expurgated* it from our Articles of Faith? After discarding Sermons XIII. and XIV. of Mr.

Wesley's as being "standard," the work would be nearly complete.

Whether we call this "corruption," the "old man," or the "body of sin," or "inbred sin," or the "infections of our nature," or "the carnal mind," or "the law of sin and death," is of little consequence; but by whatever name it is called, Paul teaches that there can be no divine or spiritual life in the soul where it remains. To say that this "infection of our nature remains in them that are regenerated," that the "former corruptions of the heart remain in the regenerate and strive for the mastery," that "the carnal mind survives the work of regeneration, and is often actively rebellious in the hearts of real Christians," to say all this, and more, is to say that Paul and Peter and John did not understand the effects of the fall and the nature of the new birth! The truth is, if a large portion of the New Testament had been written to overturn the "residue theory of regeneration," and to show that regeneration includes sanctification, the writers could scarcely have been more explicit. If there be passages that seem to teach otherwise, the contexts explain the seeming conflict. And while it is impossible to reconcile Mr. Wesley with himself, yet he always gives a Bible definition of the new birth; and if a large portion of his "Notes on the New Testament," and a larger portion of Clarke's "Commentary" had been written to overturn this "residue theory," the authors could not have used stronger language.

CHAPTER V.

The Modern Fathers in Trouble.

SECTION 1. "INSTINCTIVE CONVICTIONS."

It is amazing to see to what extent some of the modern Fathers have pressed this doctrine of "Sin in Believers" in order to make room to bring in sanctification as a "second blessing." Dr. Upham,* in his *Interior Life*," sums up "all bodily infirmities, such as disordered organs of sight, hearing, and touch," and "all mental derangements, such as unavoidable errors and imperfections of judgment," and calls them all " involuntary sins—sins though that find no recourse but in an immediate and believing application of the atoning blood." So the Doctor says: "Now,

---

*A convert of Dr. and Mrs. Palmer.

as such infirmities are very frequent, and as indeed they are unavoidable, we shall have abundant occasions to confess our trespasses!" The Doctor continues: "It is in accordance with what has now been said that Christians, . . . wherever they have fallen into such *errors and infirmities have an instinctive conviction* that the occasion is a fitting one for penitent grief and humble confession, and they find no true peace of mind until they find a sense of forgiveness!"

We presume that the Doctor is right in saying that the conviction for such "infirmities" as he describes is "an *instinctive* conviction;" at least, we have no idea that the Holy Spirit ever convicted any one for such "unavoidable infirmities," either "physical" or "intellectual." In our experience as a pastor we have met a few of the Doctor's patients who were "filled with penitent grief" on account of some physical disorder or infirmity, and whose "instinctive convictions gave them no peace of mind." We think that all such theology as the above needs medical treatment as much, or more, than the patients for whom it was prepared; and if some doctors of divinity we "wot of" had exposed the errors of Dr. Upham's writings twenty years ago, instead of recommending them to our people, they might have prevented some of the fanaticism which is now troubling the whole Church and hindering Methodism in her divine commission to "spread scriptural holiness over these lands." Now if Dr. Upham's theology be true, then it follows as a necessary sequence that, instead of our infirmities and physical disorders affording us an opportunity for developing our moral powers and Christian graces by a calm endurance and a perfect resignation, they will rob us of all "true peace of mind," and "fill us with penitent grief;" so that as by age and physical decay the hoary-headed pilgrim gradually sinks under the weight of infirmities, instead of mounting up on wings as eagles and soaring and talking with God in the land of Beulah, his "infirmities and involuntary sins" will multiply upon him, sinking him deeper and deeper in the "slough of despond," while "humble confession" becomes the only words of his mouth, and "penitential grief" the sole exercise of his pious heart!

SECTION 2. A LARGE VIEW OF THE PLAN OF SALVATION.

According to Bishop Peck in his

"*Central Idea of Christianity,*" the regenerated believer who has never forfeited his justified state must go through a second process of conviction, repentance, faith, etc., similar to that through which he entered the new life, before he can be cleansed from all sin. Of course this makes regeneration a *partial* work! The nine prerequisites, as laid down by the good Bishop, by which the partial cleansing of regeneration is to be completed are as follows: "(1) The conviction produced; (2) the resolution formed; (3) the feeling necessary; (4) the confession required; (5) the consecration made; (6) the faith exercised; (7) the prayer offered; (8) the evidence received; (9) the responsibility taken." To the discussion of these nine points the author devotes eighty-one pages, from the reading of which

I rose up involuntarily repeating, "And found no end in wandering mazes lost, vain wisdom all, and false philosophy!" If it takes that long to get from regeneration to sanctification—the "Central Idea of Christianity"—then the Bishop must have had a *large view of the plan of salvation!* The difference between Paul and Bishop Peck is that Paul in every place he uses the term sanctification, except one, puts it in immediate connection with justification, and on one occasion he puts it *first* (1 Cor. vi. 11); while the good Bishop takes eighty-one 12mo pages to get his justified believers to his central idea—moral purity! Instead of St. John taking eighty-one pages, he puts "confession," "forgiveness," and a thorough moral "cleansing from all sin" in one short verse (1 John i. 9). Surely Paul and John had a different theory of the divine life, or a different view of the "Central Idea of Christianity," or a shorter road to reach it than Bishop J. T. Peck!

SECTION 3. A NEW DEPARTURE.

If Bishop Peck were the only advocate of the theory which makes regeneration a "*partial* renovation" and sanctification a "second change," and then makes this theory the "Central Idea of Christianity," I would lay down my pen; but their name is legion, and still they come! Men and women, self-appointed and losing sight of every thing else, are giving their whole time and energies to this "Central Idea," and are calling the Church—the whole Church—to this second process of repentance, confession, and faith. Camp-meetings and conventions are being held for this specific object, at which no minister, elder, or Bishop is invited to preach or preside unless he can pronounce this Shibboleth distinctly, and, in some cases, none but justified believers are invited to the altar to "confess their sins and find true peace of mind by a believing application of the atoning blood!" Thus have things gone on until now an organization is formed which ignores and decries all Church relation, and whose self-constituted preachers travel at large in this interest and call upon all justified believers who "have an instinctive conviction that the occasion is a fitting one for penitent grief and humble confession," to "come out of the Church" that they may "find a sense of forgiveness and be sanctified." Is it not time for some one to put the brake on this "central idea" car?

That there is a great want of personal holiness in the Church, that many of her members have "left their first love," and others have "defiled their garments," and thereby have cause to confess and forsake their personal sins, that the whole Church needs a stronger faith and an increase of the spirit of prayer, I am ready to admit and deeply deplore; but I must and do, in the "fear of God and in the love of the Spirit," most respectfully enter a solemn protest against the cause assigned for these special organizations and the object proposed as being in theory or spirit any part of Bible religion, much less as being the "Central Idea of Christianity." Leaving out the *disorganizing* spirit that has already manifested itself in many places, we believe that the "residue theory of regeneration" and the "second change theory of sanctification" rest upon a false psychology and a misinterpretation of Scripture. What a fine opportunity Bishop J. S. Key had in May, 1887, when he delivered that grand sermon on "*Heart Purity*," before the "Georgia Holiness Convention," to bring out some of the historical facts I have given; but alas! like Mr. Wesley, the good Bishop was committed to the "residue theory" and the "second change theory," and this fact was known to those who invited him to preach before that Convention!

SECTION 4. SAWING OFF LIMBS.

The advocates of the "residue theory," in order to make occasion for sanctification to come after regeneration, leave something in the regenerated heart which troubles them and their theory about as much as Dr. Upham's "instinctive convictions" troubled his justified believers. Whatever it is which "remains in the heart of the regenerate," according to their own testimony, "it is not sin *proper*," for that would forfeit pardon. Yet, when they come to remove this mysterious something (which has been called by so many names), they prescribe "*conviction, repentance, confession, faith, and forgiveness!*" This looks very much like the Bible prescription for removing "sin proper." At least conviction, confession, and forgiveness" imply *guilt*, and guilt implies *condemnation!*

This confusion is worse confounded by confounding sanctification with Christian perfection, and then trying to hold on to the Bible doctrine of instantaneous sanctification. Take a case or two. In "*Perfect Love,*" page 55, Rev.

J. A. Wood says: "He who seeks the gradual attainment of entire sanctification seeks necessarily something less than entire sanctification *now*—that is, he does not seek entire sanctification *at all*. He who does not aim at the extirpation of *all sin* from his heart *now* tolerates some sin in his heart now. But he who tolerates sin in his heart is not in a condition to offer acceptable prayer to God. 'If I regard iniquity in my heart, the Lord will not hear me.'"

Now apply this sound reasoning and Bible truth to the hour of regeneration, and see how unwittingly Brother Wood has sawed off the very limb on which he stood as an advocate for "partial renovation in regeneration!" Any one can see that the "some sin tolerated in the heart of the seeker of gradual sanctification," and which prevented the Lord from hearing his prayer, is the identical sin left in his heart at regeneration and creates the necessity for sanctification as a "second cleansing!" To deny this is to give up the whole theory of "sin in believers," and leave no cause for a "second cleansing" unless justification has been forfeited by actual transgression, as it had been in David's case.

Dr. Hibbard, as quoted by Brother Wood, says: "We deny that a man ever yet gained the victory over any sin while his will retained it, even with the most secret or tacit approbation. God will have thorough work; and full salvation will never be given but on condition of entire, universal, unconditional abandonment of all sin and acceptance and approval of all the will of God.

Then, and not till then, will come the word that speaks us whole."

All this I steadfastly believe; but if applied to the sinner seeking religion, then down goes the limb on which Dr. Hibbard stands. We would like to know what kind of conditions the justified believer negotiated with the Almighty by which he retained the sins which this "second change" is to "forgive" and "cleanse." If "sin and corruption remain in the regenerate," it remains there by the assent of the will of the person regenerated, or at the will and pleasure of the Almighty; if not by the consent of the penitent, then he is in no wise responsible for it; and if by the consent of the penitent, then the Almighty must have agreed to the reservation, or he would not have "justified him freely" and renewed him in his own image. In either case the responsibility of this "remaining sin and corruption" left in the regenerate rests upon God, and not upon the "justified believer." But "God will have thorough work" in this "second change"— even "entire, universal, unconditional abandonment of all sin." The question now is: Can a man be justified and regenerated on a consecration short of "entire, universal, unconditional abandonment of all sin?" and such a consecration being made, would not the "word that speaks us *whole*" come to him then and there? If such a consecration secures sanctification, and if no man can be justified on a consecration less than that, then surely "every one who is justified is also sanctified." So Mr. Wesley was right when he made the "washing of regeneration and the renewing of the Holy Ghost include sanctification." And Dr. Clarke was right also when he said: "The new birth comprehends not only justification, but also sanctification." "If the Spirit of God dwell in you the *whole carnal mind* will be destroyed." "He is first freely justified—he feels no condemnation; he is *fully* sanctified—he walks not after the flesh, but after the Spirit."

The more we look into that theory of the Christian life which makes "regeneration a partial renovation" and "sanctification a second change," and then confounds sanctification with Christian perfection, the more we are impressed with its want of harmony with itself and the word of God. In "*Perfect Love,*" pages 55, 56, Brother Wood truly says: "To seek a gradual purity renders the attainment of entire sanctification impossible. It does so because it excludes the conditions of entire sanctification. The faith which is the proximate condition of entire sanctification can be exercised only in connection with the renunciation of all sin and complete submission to God. Conscious *confidence* and conscious *guilt* can not exist in the same heart at the same time—the former excludes the latter."

If that be true, and I believe it is true, then every one who has justifying faith has also sanctifying grace. But if "conscious confidence and conscious guilt can not exist in the same heart at the same time," how can Dr. Upham's believer, who has "instinctive *conviction*," be in a justified state? Are we to understand that "instinctive convictions" are unconscious convictions, or that the guilt which "conviction and forgiveness" imply is an unconscious guilt?

Again, if "faith can only be exercised in connection with the renunciation of all sin," how can any one exercise justifying faith without such a renunciation, and if "all sin be renounced" will not sanctification take place at justification?

Still again, if "conscious confidence and conscious guilt cannot exist in the same heart at the same time," how will Brother Wood and Bishop Peck ever make the "merely regenerate believer conscious of his remaining sin" and of his need of this "second change," without first destroying his "conscious confidence" or justifying faith?

Once more: the advocates of the

"residue theory" tell us that "the merely regenerate has remaining impurity," that "regeneration is a partial renovation," that "the former corruptions of the heart remain in them that are regenerated and strive for the mastery," that "the carnal mind survives the work of regeneration and is often in a state of active rebellion," and that "if there be no second change after justification, then we must be content to remain full of sin until death." Now, if this be the true state of the regenerated heart, is there no "conscious guilt?" If not, then how did any one ever ascertain that all this "sin and corruption remain in the regenerate" soul? But if there be "conscious guilt," and if "conscious guilt excludes conscious confidence, or faith," then all who have not received this "second change" are destitute of justifying faith; or else "conscious guilt" does not "exclude conscious confidence;" or else a man may be "full of sin and guilt," and have them both removed without ever being made "conscious" that he needed a "second change!" We insist that the advocates of the "residue theory" either abandon their theory *in toto,* or else untangle their theological hank. As an advocate of the "residue theory," no wonder Bishop J. S. Key, D.D., "*appealed for charity*" in his sermon on "Heart Purity," page 15. The case calls for all the charity that a Christian possesses; but can "charity hide such a multitude of sins" as the above catalogue, all of which are said to "remain in them that are regenerated?" Perhaps the good Bishop, when he made this "appeal for charity," was so absorbed with his theme that for the moment he overlooked the fact that the author of the thirteenth chapter of First Corinthians on one occasion "withstood Peter to the face, because he was [in error and was] to be blamed."

How much more rational and scriptural to say that every one "born of God" is "washed clean every whit;" that every one "forgiven" is "cleansed from all unrighteousness," "from all sin;" and if any one of them now has "impurity," or "is full of sin and guilt," it is because he has failed to "abide in Christ and keep his commandments," and thereby "defiled his garments."

SECTION 5. RESIDUE THEORY EXTRACTED WITH A PAIR OF BORROWED FORCEPS.

We take Brother Wood's "unanswerable argument" against sanctification being a growth, and with it we lift the "residue theory" out by the roots. In his "*Purity and Maturity,*" page 148, he says: "The fact that inbred sin is a *unit* is proof that we cannot obtain freedom from it by growth in grace. Like error, inbred sin is a simple, uncompounded element or quality, and continues unchangeably the same, at all times and under all circumstances. It cannot be analyzed, and is not subject to any changes; and in its essential nature it can never be made any thing else. Hence it *cannot be divided or subdivided and removed by parts.*"

Now this mysterious something which Brother Wood calls "inbred sin" St. Paul calls the "carnal mind," which he affirms is "enmity against God," and which Brother Wood affirms "continues unchangeably the same at all times and under all circumstances." Hence regeneration either leaves the soul in a state of "enmity against God," or else lifts "inbred sin" out by the roots; for Brother Wood truly says, "Inbred sin can not be divided or subdivided and removed by parts." So if "inbred sin" —the "carnal mind"—can not be divided and removed by parts," it is folly to talk about the "remains of the carnal mind" in a regenerated believer.

Again: All the advocates of the "residue theory" tell us that the "sin" which "remains in them that are regenerate is not 'sin proper,' which is 'a transgression of the law,' but it is the 'remains of the carnal mind'—the 'corruption of the nature of every man that is naturally engendered of the offspring of Adam'—hence it is called '*inbred sin*.'" Now every tyro in theology knows that the "standards" all teach that the "necessity of the new birth grows out of the existence of this 'inbred sin;'" so that if the new birth does not remove this "inbred sin," this "carnal mind," this natural "corruption of our nature," where is the necessity of "being born again?"

SECTION 6. A FEW FACTS; AND FACTS ARE STUBBORN THINGS.

The "higher life" to which the regenerated believer is called is a state which is reached by a proper unfolding and exercise of the graces of the "new man," and not by a second process of repentance and cleansing to remove moral corruption left in us at regeneration. To "renew, according to the [original] divine pattern in uprightness and moral purity," is truly God-like; and to use these renewed and purified powers so as not to fall into sin again, but to "perfect holiness in the fear of God," is the whole duty and the highest glory of man!

The truth is, if we make those mental states which have been called "sin in believers" the result of moral corruption, which regenerating grace could not or did not remove, we charge God with arbitrarily demanding of the regenerated believer a life of holiness when he has failed to supply him with one of the indispensable prerequisites of such a life—viz., *a pure moral nature*—and we also make regeneration a *partial* work, or else exclude from it the idea of moral renovation altogether! Which horn of this dilemma will the reader take?

The great mistake of those who have written upon the "higher life" is found in the fact that they have all confounded sanctification with Christian perfection; whereas they should have made regeneration include sanctification, and then drawn a distinction between regeneration and perfection. In regeneration the man is "created anew, according to the divine pattern, in uprightness and moral purity," and all the conditions and principles of a holy life are given; in perfection we have all these principles unfolded in the maturity of the Christian graces: the one is always complete in itself, the other exhibits different degrees of development. The divine life realized at the new birth is not two, but one. This life, like all life, is a *growth;* and this growth, like all growth, has its different *stages.*

The "residue theory" has been the source of no little trouble in Methodism for more than a century—the cause of untold difficulties to the young Christian—the mystery of orthodox theology, and more bewildering to the young preacher than the enigmatical philosophy of the Persians; and, if carried to its legitimate sequences, it would overthrow the very foundations of Christianity!

CHAPTER VI.

"Regeneration a Partial Renovation."

SECTION 1. A BRIEF REVIEW.

WE have shown that the residue theory of regeneration was expunged from our Articles of Faith. We have examined those mental states and those Scripture texts which were supposed to teach that "sin remained in them that are regenerated," and found that both could be explained without adopting the "residue theory." We have examined the Bible idea of regeneration, and found that regeneration *includes* sanctification. We have seen some of the confusion and absurdities of both Mr. Wesley and the modern Fathers in trying to harmonize their residue theory with itself and with the Bible idea of the divine life. So far we have assumed that the residue theory of necessity made regeneration a "*partial work*"—a "*partial renovation*." In this review we will let the advocates of this "theory" state their views in their own language.*

Mr. Wesley says: "If there be no second change after justification, . . . then we must remain full of sin until death."

Mr. R. Watson says: "In this regenerate state, the former corruptions of the heart may remain and strive for the mastery."

Bishop Foster says: "The merely regenerate are not entirely free from sin."

---

* Our quotations are taken from "*Perfect Love*," by Rev. J. A. Wood, a book consisting mainly of quotations from authors who hold and defend the "residue theory."

Dr. D. Curry says: "This carnal mind survives the work of regeneration, and is often actively rebellious in the hearts of real Christians."

Dr. Dick says: "Although in regeneration holy principles are infused into the soul, **yet the** *change produced is only partial.*"

Rev. J. A. Wood says: "As long as Christians live in a *partially* purified **state,**" etc. "**This** new life has existence **in a** soul *partially carnal* in the *mere* regenerate. . . . Regeneration removes *some sin or pollution.*"

Dr. J. Dempster says: "You ask, then, in what does regeneration consist? Simply in this threefold change, viz.: justification, *partial renovation,* and divine adoption."

We could multiply **such** quotations almost indefinitely, but **the** above are enough to show the *low estimate* all these authors put upon regeneration. Two of them—Brother Wood and Bishop Foster—speak of those who have been "born of the Spirit," have been "made *partakers* of Christ," "of the Holy Ghost," "of the divine nature," "created anew in righteousness and true holiness"—they speak of such as the "*mere* regenerate." Dr. Dick says "the *change* produced is only *partial*," and Dr. Dempster says it is "simply a *partial renovation*." There it is: "MERE REGENERATION SIMPLY CONSISTS IN A PARTIAL CHANGE, A PARTIAL RENOVATION!" What will Mr. Orthodoxy think and say of all this? Surely he has been on a journey, or taking a nap, while these modern Fathers have been dressing up this "new man?" With the "carnal mind still surviving the death throes of crucifixion and in a state of active rebellion," with "the former corruptions of the heart still remaining and striving for the mastery," he looks more like St. Paul's "old man" crying out, "Who shall deliver me from the body of this death?" than St. Paul's "*new man which is created after the divine pattern in uprightness and moral purity.*"

Now this residue theory is either the "remains of Antinomianism in our Arminian theology," or else it is a twin brother thereof, and had its origin in a misinterpretation of St. Paul's Epistles. The application of the seventh chapter of Romans to a regenerated man is no greater perversion of Scripture than is made in trying to prove the residue theory by proof-texts and Scripture examples! And the analogy does not stop at this; for when this "residue theory" gets fixed in the mind of a man, I had as soon try to explain the seventh chapter of Romans to an Antinomian Calvinist as to reason with him. Hence, my object in writing these pages is not to convert any one who holds the "residue theory," but to relieve those who are bewildered by the absurdities involved in this theory, and to show all concerned that a man may reject the "residue theory" and still be in accord with our Articles of Faith and in harmony with our "standards," so far as they are in harmony with themselves and the plain teaching of the Bible.

SECTION 2. AN IMPORTANT DISCOVERY.

We would start the young convert, the newborn soul, and the reclaimed backslider exactly on the same plane of moral *purity* which is claimed for one who has received this "second change." St. John's theory of the divine life is: "If we confess our sins, he is faithful and just to forgive us our sins and to cleanse us from *all* unrighteousness. . . . My little children, these things write I unto you, that ye sin not. And if any man sin, we have an Advocate with the Father, Jesus Christ the righteous; and he is the propitiation for our sins; and not for ours only, but also for the sins of the whole world." (1 John i. 9; ii. 1; 2.) In this theory *entire* sanctification—a "cleansing from *all unrighteousness*"—follows "forgiveness;" and the "second cleansing" was contingent upon such a man "committing sin," and not because "regeneration is a *partial renovation—a partial change.*"

Dr. T. O. Summers truly says: "Regeneration is an instantaneous work—it admits of no degrees, of no progression. We can not be partially regenerated—we are, or are not, born again." As justification cancels the *guilt* of sin, so regeneration removes the *corruption* of sin. God can no more cleanse us in *part* than he can forgive us in *part*. Hence Dr. Summers says: "It is certain that regeneration extends to our *whole* moral nature. In the new birth the tone, the temper, and *tendency* of our minds are changed; the *current* of our feelings is made to run in a different channel, and the *capacity* to do the will of God is imparted." (Dr. T. O. Summers on *Holiness*.)

What the Doctor here calls a "capacity to do the will of God" is what we mean by the conditions and principles of holiness, and what Paul means by "putting on the new man, which is created according to the divine pattern in uprightness and moral purity." Such a man is at one with his Maker—"created anew in the image of God"—with the "Holy Spirit to dwell in him and guide him into all truth." But while in the first stages of the Christian life all those mental states which have been mistaken for the "remains of the carnal mind" and the "motions of inbred sin," will, more or less, enter into his experience; yet, in their *origin*, they are nothing more than the power of temptation made doubly strong by old habits; and while we fear that many—nearly all—yield now and then to temptation and commit sin—"defile their garments"—yet there is no moral necessity for it. Every one "born of

God" might "go" right "on to perfection" by "*abiding* in Christ and keeping his commandments."

While perfection is a "higher life" than regeneration, yet this "higher life" is nothing more than the *pure* babe in Christ *developed* into a *mature* man or woman in Christ Jesus; together with the moral *character* which is superinduced by a retroaction from the activity involved in the conflict with evil in maintaining a *pure* heart and a *justified* state. "Sin is not a *substance* but an *act;* not a *thing existing*, but a thing *done;*" and moral corruption is a *retroaction* which supervenes upon this voluntary wrong act, *inducing a wrong state of our moral powers. Vice versa*, virtue is not a substance, but an act; not a thing existing, but a thing done; and holiness is the result, or the retroaction, of voluntary right action. Now God supplies all the essential conditions* of holiness, and we are to "perfect holiness in the fear of God" "by abiding in Christ and keeping his commandments"—by "abiding in him and sinning not."

We should never forget that the possession of all the moral faculties in a *pure* state and the possession of holiness are two distinct things. The essential conditions of a moral agent being given, the self-active power of the will, together with the reflex actions of the will, are the origin and cause of all virtue and holiness, all sin and moral corruption in man. If this metaphysical and psychological postulate be constantly kept in mind, then all will be

---

'*These conditions are intelligence, moral freedom, moral purity, and a rule of life—a law.

clear; but if it be overlooked or ignored, then we are without chart or compass, driving into a darker sea at every plunge! Now, one of the indispensable prerequisites of a moral agent in order to holy living is a *pure* moral nature to begin with; hence, God created Adam *pure*—free from all moral taint. *We have now discovered the true* PHILOSOPHY OF THE CHRISTIAN LIFE, *which unfolds to us the* NATURE *and* EXTENT *of* REGENERATION. In arranging the plan of salvation God saw that in the very nature of things justification would be of no avail to fallen, corrupt man, unless his moral nature was "*purified*" and "*renewed in the image of him who created him;*" so God provided means by which, in every case where he forgives sins, then and there he "*cleanses us from* ALL UNRIGHTEOUSNESS," *and* "*creates us anew* *according to the [original] divine pattern in* UPRIGHTNESS *and* MORAL PURITY."* *So that every one who is justified is also "*FULLY SANCTIFIED.*"*

So patent is this fact, that Dr. Summers says: "Justification without sanctification would be of no advantage to us. What if our sins were pardoned—what if we were restored to the favor of God? If our hearts were not renewed and our lives regulated by the Spirit of grace, we should forfeit our justification as soon as received; we should involve ourselves immediately in guilt and condemnation. To retain the divine favor we must be born again." ("Holiness," page 22.) Observe, Dr. Summers not only uses the terms

---

* If any prefer, they may read "in righteousness and true holiness"—the other is a better translation of Eph. iv. 24.

"born again," "renewed," and "sanctification," to express the same work of grace, but he also declares that the work of grace expressed by these terms must immediately follow justification; else "we should forfeit our justification as soon as received." When Dr. Summers wrote the above paragraph he knew that Mr. Wesley had said: "To be born again is to be *inwardly changed from all sinfulness to all holiness.*" And that Dr. Clarke had said: "Sin must be pardoned, and the *impurity* of the heart *washed away* before any soul can possibly enter into the kingdom of God. This new birth implies the renewing of the *whole* soul in righteousness and true holiness." "He is first freely justified—he feels no condemnation; he is FULLY *sanctified*—he walks not after the flesh, but after the Spirit."

SECTION 3. ANALYZING CHRISTIAN EXPERIENCE IN A PSYCHOLOGICAL CRUCIBLE.

We are now prepared to examine the experience of those who have professed to have "obtained sanctification as a second change, cleansing them from all sin." The facts can all be accounted for from our stand-point and reconciled with our theory of the divine life. That they had a consciousness of inward corruption after regeneration, and before they received the "second blessing," may be true; but whence came this consciousness of impurity? Did it originate in the supposed fact that "regeneration is a partial renovation," or in the fact that they mistook a severe temptation—the uprising of desire under enticement—for "the remains of the carnal mind," the "motions of inbred sin," or in the fact that they failed at some point to "fulfill the righteousness of the law by walking after the flesh, and not after the Spirit?" We do not accuse them of "denying the faith," nor of having given up their "original purpose to serve God and get to heaven," but of having failed in the discharge of some duty, or having yielded to some temptation and of committing some sin; and every sin, whether of omission or of commission, leaves a stain of moral corruption. Now, if a sinner who has never "tasted of the heavenly gift" has deep compunctions of conscience in the hour of conviction and repentance, how much more they who have sinned against the light of Christian experience? When David was in such deep agony, and prayed for a "clean heart" and a "renewed spirit," he was a backslider, and not a "*partially renovated*" convert. When Christians pass through such a crucible, and are restored to moral purity, it would be strange if they did not profit by such an experience—especially if they begin to seek this restoration with the idea fixed in their minds that it is their privilege to be "cleansed from all sin," and then to "abide in Christ and sin not." But how much better for them if they had been told at regeneration that they were "forgiven and cleansed from all unrighteousness," being "created anew according to the divine pattern in uprightness and moral purity," and that they might go right on to perfection by "abiding in Christ and keeping his commandments."

We do not deny, but believe, that thousands have sought sanctification as a "second blessing," and that they were then and there sanctified—"cleansed from all unrighteousness," "from all sin "—but that does *not prove* that they were not "cleansed from all unrighteousness" when they were first "forgiven." Not at all; for according to John such a "forgiveness" and "cleansing" go hand in hand, and he pledges the "faithfulness and justice" of God to this order in their reception. (1 John i. 9.)

We should be very careful how we adopt every theory of the divine life which may claim to be evolved from Christian experience. When we remember that not one man in every thousand is capable of so analyzing his own mental states as to give any correct theory of mental philosophy, it behooves us to go slow in forming a "*theory*" of the Christian life from *data* gathered from what men say they have experienced; not but what they are honest, but because so few are capable of so *analyzing* and *classifying* their mental states and feelings as to give *data for such a purpose.* We know as an historical fact that some of the first who professed to have obtained sanctification as a "second change," in less than a week after Mr. Wesley had accepted the theory on their testimony, began to testify that they had "received a third change or blessing which raised them above temptation," etc.; and to meet this fanaticism Mr. Wesley wrote and published his sermon on "Sin in Believers."

There is a wide difference between *analyzing* and *classifying* known facts until they crystallize into a "theory," and *assuming* a "theory" and then trying to find facts to sustain it. It is very easy to *assume* that "regeneration is a partial renovation," leaving "inbred sin" and a "residue of the carnal mind in the regenerated heart," and then appeal to the *consciousness* of the average Church-member, and get a verdict from thousands in favor of *conscious impurity*, especially when learned doctors have mistaken the mental excitement caused by a severe temptation for the "carnal mind in a state of active rebellion!" But put all the facts into a *psychological crucible and analyze them in the light of God's word*, and we find that they were "*cleansed every whit,*" when they were "washed in the laver of regeneration and renewed by the Holy Ghost;" and that the reason they now have a consciousness of impurity arises from a mistaken idea of the mental states involved in temptation, or from the fact that they have "left their first love" and "defiled their garments."

The old Antinomian idea, that it is necessary for us to sin all through life, and that all sins committed after justification are to be charged up to the "old man," and not to the "new man"—I say this old Antinomian, Calvinistic idea of the Christian life has been greatly strengthened in the minds of our people by those who are always teaching that "regeneration is a *partial* renovation," leaving the "carnal mind in a state of active rebellion," and that all this "remaining corruption" and "heart impurity" is *compatible with a justified state!* We do not charge such teachers with impure motives, but with *error*, and a "zeal not according to knowledge." When holiness becomes a hobby, and is ridden in the interest of an independent organization, it is time the Church of Christ should rescue it from such a position and give it its proper place in her teachings. I deal not with motives—I leave that to the Master—but with facts and teachings and their palpable influences and issues. I think the salvation provided in the gospel is a *unit—entire, indivisible, perfect.*

SECTION 4. OFFERING STRANGE FIRE ON METHODIST ALTARS—A NEW DEPARTURE.

The reader of these pages may have regarded some of my criticisms too severe; but having read every thing that I could find in book form and a vast amount of periodical literature on this subject, my diagnosis of the case was: it calls for heroic treatment. In the *Texas Christian Advocate* of October 6, 1887, I find an article of nearly three columns on "*sanctification as taught by John Wesley,*" written by Rev. A. H. Sutherland in reply to some brother who had dared to express his views and doubts about the "residue theory of regeneration and the second change theory of sanctification." After quoting the usual paragraphs from Mr. Wesley—paragraphs that have been quoted so much that some editors and proof-readers must have learned them all by rote long ago—Brother Sutherland proceeds to make the following appeal and denunciation:

"Therefore, why oppose those who are doing exactly what Mr. Wesley did and enjoined? Why do you not do that way? Because you do not believe that way? Then why continue in a Church whose most distinctive, distinguished, and glorious doctrine you reject? Why come to her altars to offer your *strange fire*? Why stand around her tables for your bread? I declare to you there is distinctiveness in your doctrine to justify a new Church; for there is no Church on earth that holds it as a tenet. No Church—no, not one besides the Methodist—believes in entire sanctification before death. Nor does she believe it to be co-etaneous with justification and regeneration and the new birth. You enjoy the distinction—which is no honor—of being a class, almost a party, in a Church which believes that which is not yet a creed, and of teaching that which your Church emphatically condemns (?). Brethren, take my advice, suffer the word of exhortation; retrace your steps, re-read your standards, be converted from the error of your ways [and then seek the second change], or quietly withdraw from *our* Church with *our* tears and *our* prayers."

On this remarkable appeal, denunciation, declamation, and exhortation, so beautifully combined and interspersed with "prayers" and suffused with "tears," I have a few points to make. 1. No one can analyze the document without seeing that with Brother Sutherland to oppose the "residue *theory* of regeneration and the second change *theory* of sanctification" is to oppose *sanctification itself*. In other words, Brother Sutherland has things so confused that he can not draw the distinction between rejecting *his theory* of sanctification and rejecting the *doctrine* of sanctification. To deny this criticism is to make him write nonsense; and to admit the truth and justice of the criticism is to say that Brother Sutherland was fighting a man of straw. There is no use in reasoning with a man who can not distinguish between a certain *theory* of a doctrine and the doctrine itself. Hence, I have already said that I have no hope of converting such a man—no, not if I could reason like Lord Bacon, and exhort like Rev. A. H. Sutherland, and weep like Jeremiah the prophet. 2. When Brother Sutherland said that those who reject the residue theory " enjoyed the *distinction—*which is *no honor*—of being a class in a Church who believe that which is *not yet* a creed," did he know that we enjoyed both the *distinction* and the *honor* of being in a Church from whose *Creed* this same " residue theory," which we reject, was *expunged by Mr. Wesley's own hand?* If he did, was he not a *little* hasty when he in " tears " invited us to "quietly *withdraw* from the Church" for rejecting an *expurgated* theory? If he did not know this historical fact, would not an "exhortation to re-read our standards," and add a *little* Church history and the Articles of Faith to the course be well timed, especially as it might save the good brother a good many imaginary "tears" by removing the hypothetical cause? 3. When Brother Sutherland said that those who hold and teach that regeneration and sanctification are co-etaneous, "are teaching that which our *Church emphatically condemns*," did he know that in teaching thus we were in perfect *accord* with our expurgated Articles of Faith as prepared by Wesley himself; that we were in *accord* with our "standard authors" so far as they are in harmony with themselves; and that we were in perfect *accord* with the word of God, especially as that word is expounded in Mr. Wesley's "Notes" and Clarke's "Commentary?" If he did know all this, what did he mean, and to whom did he refer, when he said the "Church emphatically condemns" such "teaching?" And what did he mean by calling such teaching "offering strange fire" on the "altars" of our Church? But if he was ignorant of these facts, instead of "re-reading our standards," I think he had better *read* them. 4. After showing that there were *some* in the Methodist Episcopal Church, South, who rejected *his theory* of sanctification, he asks (not in "tears"), "Why then continue in a Church whose most *distinctive, distinguished, and glorious doctrine you reject?*" Reject what? The "glorious doctrine of sanctification?" Nay, my brother, only your *theory of it*—that is all! Does Brother Sutherland really know that the "distinctive, distinguished, and glorious doctrine" of *genuine* Methodism is "a *present, full salvation from all sin, by faith in* Christ"— thus ignoring the Romish purgatory *after* death, and the Calvinistic purgatory *in* death, and the residue purgatory *of* the second change theory; and that in rejecting the residue theory *in toto* we are only doing for our theory of the divine life what Mr. Wesley did for our Creed. Because Mr. Wesley, as a loyal, consistent minister of the Church of England, accepted the residue theory as taught in her Ninth Article; and because Mr. Wesley struggled with the absurdities of this theory for forty years, until finally he rejected it so far as to *expunge* it from the Articles of Faith prepared for American Methodists, shall we now turn round and put our necks under this "yoke which neither we nor our fathers were able to bear?"

5. But Brother Sutherland reaches his climax when he says, "I declare there is distinctiveness in your doctrine to justify a new Church!" There is no difference among us about *doctrine*—we all believe alike in the **doctrine** of sanctification—the only difference is whether the Bible teaches a *full salvation from all sin now,* or a *partial cleansing now, and a complete cleansing at some future time!* It is not sanctification, but your *theory of it,* we reject. This is not all: If any have "tears" to shed, they need not save them until we "quietly withdraw from the Church" and organize "a new Church," for that will never be. Those who are read up in the history of Meth-

odism **know** that **the** "withdrawing" began, and has continued so far, among **those** who are on **the** other side of this "theory." It was George **Bell,** Thomas Maxfield, and others, who were among the *first* to profess sanctification as **a** "second change," and upon whose *testimony* Mr. **Wesley** accepted this theory, who were also the *first* to "withdraw" and set up for themselves. **It is** this same "class," or "party,"* **who have** "quietly," or otherwise, "withdrawn from the Church" **in** the North-west and organized a force and sent them out to go everywhere and cry, "*Come out of the Church!*" some of whom have "made havoc among the Churches" in Alabama. It is this same "class," or "party," who have organized all the

---

*I am indebted to Brother Sutherland for these terms.

"Holiness Conventions" that are now operating in this country on an *independent* line! And if there ever is to be a *general* "withdrawing from the Church," and "a new Church organized" on account of this "residue theory," it does not take a prophet to tell where the "withdrawing" will begin, and which "class or party" now "in the Church" will compose the "new Church." I thought I saw that this issue was coming before I began to write these pages, and my first object was to arrest this tendency. But Brother Sutherland has raised the issue while I am writing; but to my surprise, instead of following the example of Messrs. Bell and Maxfield, he politely asks us to "quietly withdraw from *our* Church with *our* tears and *our* prayers!" As this is "a new departure" in Methodist history, we ask for time to consider the proposition. In the meantime, we hope Brother Sutherland and *all his* "party in the Church" will read and "*re*-read our standards," and refer now and then to Methodist history and "*our*" Articles of Faith.*

---

*There is no article on sanctification among the twenty-five articles of the Methodist creed. There is no allusion to the doctrine or statement as to what we shall believe about it. Sanctification is not a doctrine, but an experience, and when it is presented simply as purity of heart and life before God, it finds none to oppose it, none to cavil at it. To be holy is a duty confessed by all Christians, and it is agreed we should own no model or pattern lower than the Great Exemplar. While we point out men's sins, and urge them to put them away, none can gainsay our teachings. While we urge that no known sin should be harbored or indulged, all Christians agree with us. It is only when some one puts forward his theory of the operations of divine grace, or puts himself forward as an illustration of a particular work of grace, that confusion and contradictions arise. As respects the model to which we should conform our lives, it is found in Him alone who says, "Learn of me." To any one who thrusts himself between us and this perfect light, claiming himself to be an example of perfection, we will say, as Diogenes said to Alexander, "Stand out of my sunshine."—*South-western Methodist.*

CHAPTER VII.
Christian Perfection.

OUR object has not been to lower the standard of Christian experience or holy living, but to remove some of the difficulties which have gathered around both, and to place each where the inspired writers left them. We would start the young convert and the reclaimed backslider on exactly the same plane of Christian experience which is claimed for one who has received the "second change." As the whole subject is usually presented, no wonder so few "go on to perfection," and so many get into trouble and confusion. Sanctification is not a growth in grace, but an act of cleansing which prepares the newborn soul to grow. It takes the moral purity of sanctification and a growth in grace to mature into perfection. The young Christians who fail to see all this fail to maintain a pure heart, and for the want of a pure heart they fail to grow; and for the want of a pure heart, and the growth that would follow, they fail to "go on unto perfection."

SECTION 1. "GROWING OUT OF SIN."

As the word of God requires purity of heart and a growth in grace, some have concluded that they could grow out of sin into moral purity. Now moral purity is not a question of time, but a growth in grace is. There is no such thing as a gradual growing out of sin; for sin is not a thing to be outgrown, but an act to be forgiven and a stain to be washed away. The guilt of sin must be forgiven and the pollution of sin must be washed away by faith in the blood of the Lamb; and all this is an instantaneous work. A full salvation from all sin is the present privilege of all who "believe with a heart unto righteousness." There is such a thing as growth in unfolding the Christian graces, which growth results in Christian perfection; but the simple act of sanctification—of being "cleansed from all sin"—is a work of the Holy Spirit performed in the "washing of regeneration."

In the *Methodist Quarterly Review* for July, 1877, Rev. J. O. A. Clarke, D.D., LL.D., truly says: "Every believer whose sins are truly forgiven, and who is begotten of God, is *pure* in heart, *free* from sin, and *sanctified*. And this sanctification is contemporaneous with the new creation. For 'God from the beginning (that is, from the believer's hearing and obeying the gospel) hath chosen him to salvation through the sanctification of the Spirit and belief of the truth.' When 'old things are passed away, and all things become new,' the believer is sanctified, freed from sin, and 'becomes a servant of God.' From that moment he is one of the 'elect of God the Father, through sanctification of the Spirit unto obedience and sprinkling of the blood of Jesus Christ.'" Dr. Clarke is equally clear in reference to the true position of Christian perfection in the divine life. He says: "What is perfection? and where does it begin? It is *relative*, and because it is relative it begins as soon as the believer is created anew in Christ Jesus. In the new creation he is made as perfect in moral character as it is possible for him *then* to be. He can be no more or less perfect than he is made at the time by the sanctifying Spirit. . . . Now what of Christian perfection after the new birth? We answer: It is living in obedience to the constitution and laws of the new man in Christ Jesus. And what are these? They may be summed up in a single word, and that word is *growth*. It is 'going on unto perfection.'" The Doctor goes on to show that every thing in the Word of God with which the Christian life is compared denotes progress and growth. It is a "journey, a pilgrimage, a voyage, a warfare, a race." It is "likened to a grain of mustard-seed, which grew into a tree;" to the "leaven which leavens the whole lump;" to a "babe" which is to become a "man in Christ Jesus." But as in nature, there comes a state of *maturity*, and that state of maturity is called Christian perfection.

SECTION 2. PURITY AND MATURITY.

We must remember that purity and maturity are not the same. Purity is the result of *cleansing*; maturity is the result of *growth*. The justified believer, the newborn soul, is "cleansed from all unrighteousness," is sanctified by the "washing of regeneration and the renewing of the Holy Ghost;" but he is not a mature Christian, for that implies *time, experience, and growth*. The Bible teaches a gradual maturity; but when God cleanses a soul, he says: "I will; be thou clean," and the *work is done!* A full salvation from all sin is the present and constant privilege of all who are in Christ and abide in him; and all who thus abide in him are prepared for a rapid, solid growth in grace. "He that abideth in me, and I in him, the same bringeth forth much fruit."

The powers of the soul may be developed and the Christian graces may be unfolded in a *pure* heart. Purity in quality does not exclude increase in quantity. "Water in a small channel may be just as pure as in a large one. A pure stream may increase in volume and power. Mere growth never changes the nature of any thing—that which is pure may grow, or that which is impure may grow." The worst sinner grows most rapidly in hellish passions, and the best Christian grows most rapidly in heavenly virtues and the Christian graces. Growth is natural; the act of cleansing a soul is *super*-natural and instantaneous. Every change effected by growth relates to quantity or to size; every change effected by cleansing relates to quality or to kind. To be cleansed from all sin is a work to be done by the Spirit, acting directly upon the soul; but to bring the Christian graces to the highest state of maturity is a work of time to be carried on to the day of Jesus Christ.

The whole object of the gospel is to make man *pure* and *keep* him pure. As "inbred sin" is derived from Adam, the first man, so in the new birth righteousness is derived from Christ, our second Adam; for the "new man is created according to the [original] divine pattern in righteousness and true holiness;" so that, "as we have borne the image of the earthly, we may also bear the image of the heavenly." "Now ye are clean through the word I have spoken unto you. Abide in me, and I in you." "If ye keep my commandments, ye shall abide in my love;" and "he that abideth in Christ sinneth not." Such is the philosophy of a holy life. "Whoso keepeth his word, in him verily is the *love* of God *perfected.*" Here is "*perfect love,*" and the way to attain it and keep it. Yet Rev. J. A. Wood wrote a book of three hundred and fourteen pages to show that perfect love could be attained only by a "second process of repentance and faith after regeneration;" when St. John in the very text where Brother Wood got the title of his book, affirms that "*whoso keepeth his word, in him verily is the* LOVE *of God* PERFECTED!"

SECTION 3. CONFUSION OF CONFOUNDING TERMS WHICH ARE DISTINCT.*

Those who hold that sanctification is a "second change" have done much to

---

* Of all the books I have read, "Perfect Love" and "Purity and Maturity," by Rev. J. A. Wood, excel in this work of confusion.

strengthen the idea that sanctification is to be reached by a growth. It is done in this way: In order to prove that sanctification is distinct from regeneration, they confound sanctification with Christian perfection (which is reached by a growth); and then their proof-texts lead their readers to the conclusion that whatever this "second change" may be, they are to reach it by a growth in grace. Purity is sanctification, and maturity is Christian perfection; now think of a man writing a book to show that "sanctification and perfection are the *same* thing," and then writing another book to show that "purity and maturity stand forth in Bible teaching as *distinct*," and you have the feat which Rev. J. A. Wood has accomplished! The idea that a new-born soul may become a mature Christian in a moment is more than most minds can comprehend; yet this is the case if "sanctification and Christian perfection are *synonymous*—pointing to the *same* state." And Brother Wood's ingenious effort to conceal this absurdity in his theory of Christian experience, by changing terms, is too glaring to escape the notice of any mind that is not blinded by a pet theory.

Now the Bible theory is this: The newborn soul is as pure as the blood of Christ can cleanse it, and this babe in Christ is to become a mature Christian by growing in grace. This confounding sanctification with perfection—purity with maturity—has led thousands to believe that between regeneration and sanctification there was an indefinite period of gradual development, and that after sanctification is reached the whole object of Christian experience and life was accomplished; and all they have to do after being sanctified is to find a sentimental sofa, provided for the sanctified on their way to heaven, where they may take a seat and chant,

> "My willing soul would stay
> In such a frame as this,
> And sit and sing itself away
> To everlasting bliss!"

or, seeing that they can not be made free from sin until they are sanctified, and believing that they can not reach sanctification without a life-time to grow in grace, they *content* themselves with the fact that they have been converted, and that their original purpose to serve God and get to heaven still remains, and that they intend to hold on to the Church and limp along somehow until they become men or women in Christ

Jesus; then they will "crucify the old man," which has held them in bondage so long, and "destroy the body of sin" which has been, as a mass of moral corruption, fastened upon them. Thus thousands live either in a state of contemplative *inactivity*—a sentimental *quietism*—or in a state of spiritual darkness and condemnation for years, with nothing left but the memory of their past conversion and their original purpose to serve God and get to heaven!

Now if all these could be made to see and realize that there is no Christian *life* that does not free us from sin; that "if any man sin we have an advocate with the Father;" that "if we confess our sins, he is faithful and just to forgive us our sins and to cleanse us from all unrighteousness;" and that "whosoever abideth in him sinneth not"—then we might begin to talk about a *"pure Church, without spot, or wrinkle, or blemish, or any such thing!"* But so long as a great many of our ministers believe and preach and publish to the world that the "regenerate have remaining impurity," or that the "former corruptions of the heart remain in them and strive for the mastery," or that the "carnal mind survives the work of regeneration, and remains in the heart in a state of active rebellion," and that all this may abide or exist "in *real Christians*" without justification being forfeited, so long will the vast majority of those who "have been once enlightened and have tasted of the good word of God, and the powers of the world to come," be indifferent to the calls to a "higher life." The time has come when every true watchman upon the walls of

Zion must proclaim that there is no spiritual life which does not "cleanse us from all sin;" that there is no "new man" unless he has been "created according to the [original] divine pattern in righteousness and true holiness;" that "whosoever abideth in him sinneth not," and whosoever hath sin abiding in him hath "departed from the living God" and "defiled his garments;" that "he that doeth righteousness is righteous, even as he is righteous," and "he that committeth sin is of the devil;" and that the "higher life" is reached by "keeping ourselves in the love of God, building up ourselves on our most holy faith, praying in the Holy Ghost," and "looking unto him that is able to keep us from falling," "praying always with all prayer and supplication in the Spirit, and watching thereunto with all perseverance," "till we all come in the unity of the faith, and of the knowledge of the Son of God, unto perfect men, unto the measure of the stature of the fullness of Christ, and grow up into him in all things, who is the Head of the Church." Such is the "higher life" to which every babe in Christ is called, and such is the means by which he is to attain it.

SECTION 4. HOLINESS—PERFECT LOVE—PERFECT FAITH—PERFECTION.

So far from it being impossible for a sanctified Christian to grow in grace, *moral purity* is one of the indispensable *laws* of spiritual life and growth. We have seen that regeneration *includes* sanctification—that "to be born of God is to be changed from *all* inward sinfulness to *all* inward holiness." A soul that is pure possesses a *nature* from which holiness proceeds. While holiness and perfection presupposes a *pure* moral nature, yet all the Bible teaches of holiness and perfection as a duty enjoined or a state to be reached, relates to the practical part of Christian life and experience. The Holy Spirit purifies our moral nature, and we are to purify our lives. Hence, Paul says: "Let us cleanse ourselves from all filthiness of the flesh and spirit, perfecting holiness in the fear of God." The work of "cleansing" and "perfecting holiness" is here enjoined upon *us as our work*. Now, no one can "cleanse" his moral nature; but he can "cleanse" his life; and in so doing, he will be "perfecting holiness." Regeneration, born of the Spirit, created anew, and sanctification, are all applied to the act by which man's moral nature is purified and renewed in the divine image; while "perfect love," "holiness," and "perfection" are applied to that life of obedience which results in Christian maturity. A failure to observe the distinction between what God does for us and what we are to do for ourselves has created no little confusion among those who have written upon the "higher life." The one is the divine side of the Christian life, the other is the human side. As repentance toward God and faith in our Lord Jesus Christ is sure to be followed by the "forgiveness of our sins" and a "cleansing from all unrighteousness," so obedience is sure to be followed by a pure life, a growth in grace, and a maturity of the fruits of the Spirit.

If we are not mistaken in the signs of the times, there is a growing tendency to run the "higher life" into a state of mere contemplation. This is one of the legitimate results of that theory which confounds sanctification with perfection—purity with maturity. It is easy to comprehend how a soul may be "cleansed from all sin" in a moment, for that is the work of the Spirit; but how a babe in Christ can become a man in Christ Jesus by a single act of faith is not so easily comprehended; and where such a theory is lodged in the mind it paralyzes all Christian activity, and produces an abnormal state of mere contemplation.

Our proper work as "new creatures" is to "abide in Christ and keep his commandments"—to "grow in grace" and "go on to perfection." Hence every itinerant preacher is asked at the door of the Conference: "Have you faith in Christ? Are you going on to perfection? Do you expect to be made perfect in love in this life? Are you groaning after it?"* The way to obtain "perfect love" is obedience: "Whoso keepeth his word, in him verily is the love of God perfected." The way to "perfect holiness" is to "cleanse ourselves"—our lives—"from all filthiness of the flesh and spirit." The way to "perfect faith" is by good works: "Seest thou how faith wrought with his works, and *by works* was faith made perfect." The command is, "Be ye holy." How? "As ye have yielded your members servants to uncleanness and to iniquity unto iniquity, even so now yield

---

* No man would quote these vows to prove that sanctification is a "second change," if he had not first confounded sanctification with Christian perfection—purity with maturity.

your members servants to righteousness unto holiness;" for "now being made free from sin, and become servants of God, ye have your fruit unto holiness." With the Bible before him, how any man can propose to write a book and say, "In this work I shall use the terms sanctification, perfect love, holiness, maturity, and perfection, as meaning the same thing, and as describing the same work of grace in the heart," is a mystery I can not comprehend! And yet all the books on the "higher life" are written from this stand-point. Is it any wonder that those who wrote them and those who read them "find no end in wandering mazes lost?" Is it any wonder that under such teachers the very terms "sanctification," "holiness," and "Christian perfection" have become the synonyms of "confusion," "mystery," and "fanaticism?" And what is worse than all is, if a man has a mind that can write a book on a proposition so absurd as that, without discovering the absurdity, there is but little hope of ever getting him to see how absurd such an absurdity really is. If any one thinks this is severe, all I ask is, get the "*Southern Methodist Review*" for November, 1887, and read the article on "*Sanctification.*"

The importance of purifying our lives as God purifies our hearts, in order to "perfect holiness in the fear of God," has not been fully realized by the Church; and nothing tends more to call off the mind of the Church from this important duty than to confound sanctification with Christian perfection. Those who make this mistake gather up a number of proof-texts without any reference to the contexts; just so the word *sanctify,* or *perfection,* or *holiness,* occurs in the text, they seem never to stop to see the nature of the duty enjoined, or the true application of the word used. To them they all have the same meaning and look to the same end; and that end is a "second change" to remove "remaining corruption," which they imagine was left in the moral nature of those who have been "renewed in the divine image" and "made partakers of the divine nature."

The holiness required of us in the Bible is more than "a *state* of moral purity," or "the right *state* of our powers," or "the right *temper* of our minds," or "the right *disposition* of our souls" —holiness is more than all these negative virtues and necessitated states of the soul, which culminate in "doing no harm." God will supply us with all the prerequisites to holiness (such as freedom from the guilt and pollution of sin, a *pure* moral nature, and the indwelling Spirit); but we must "*walk* after the Spirit," "be *led* by the Spirit," be "*taught* of the Spirit"—we must "*fulfill* the righteousness of the law," and "cleanse ourselves from all filthiness of the flesh and spirit, perfecting holiness in the fear of God."

A command to do is as much a law as a command not to do; and a violation of the one command is as much a sin as the violation of the other. The servant of one talent was called a "wicked servant," not because he had used it to do evil, but because he had failed to improve it. The fig-tree was cursed, not because it bore pernicious fruit, but because it bore *no* fruit. The inhabitants of **Meroz** were " cursed **bitterly,**" not because they **went** over and joined the enemy, but "because they *came not* up to the help of the **Lord,** to the help of the Lord against the mighty." " How shall we escape if we *neglect* so great **salvation?**" Christ represents many as being condemned at the judgment because of duties neglected. The possibility and **the duty of a** Christian " **abiding in Christ** and sinning not "— of " abiding in him **and** keeping his **commandments**"—is the grand question we wish to get before the Church. A Christian life which produces *obedience* is the " higher life " to which we are called. A *pure* heart, followed by a *holy* life, is the **gr**a**nd** end proposed in the gospel.

But it seems **more** reasonable to many that Christ can " cleanse **us from** all sin" than that we can be "preserved blameless" in such a state. That is, they can see how Christ can do his part, but they do not see how we are to perform our part. Of course, if left to our own strength we would fail; but the grace which renews us in the divine image and purifies our hearts can sustain us. John says: "Whosoever is born of God doth not commit sin; for his seed remaineth in him: and he can not sin, because he is born of God." (1 John iii. 9.) In the new birth we are "renewed in the image of him who created us," we "put off the old man, which is corrupt, and put on the new man, which is created according to the [original] divine pattern in uprightness and moral purity;" "we are made partakers of the divine nature," "being born, not of corruptible seed, but of incorruptible, by the word of God." Now "that which is born of the Spirit is spirit," and this spiritual nature is the "*seed*" which "remains in those who are born of God"—this is the "law of the Spirit of life in Christ Jesus, which makes us free from the law of sin and death"—this "destroys the body of sin," "the carnal mind," and gives us a "spiritual mind," "if so be that the Spirit of God dwells in you." Now the indwelling of this "*seed*" is an infallible *preventive* of the commission of sin. Such a man "doth not commit sin, for his seed remaineth in him, and he can not sin because he is born of God." This state is maintained by "abiding in Christ;" "whoso *abideth* in him *sinneth not;*" for if we "abide in him," his "seed will remain in us;" and so long as "his seed remaineth in us we can not sin, because we are born of God"—we have the "Spirit of life in Christ Jesus," which "frees us from the law of sin and death," so "that the righteousness of the law is fulfilled in us." A holy life depends, then, upon our "being born of God," and "abiding in Christ." "Abide in me, and I in you. As the branch can not bear fruit of itself, except it abide in the vine, no more can ye, except ye abide in me. I am the vine, ye are the branches. He that abideth in me, and I in him, the same bringeth forth much fruit; for *without me ye can do nothing.*" The question now is, how are we to "abide in Christ?" The *bond* of this union with Christ is *faith*. Paul says: "The just shall live by *faith;*" "we walk by *faith;*" "thou standeth by *faith;*" "the life I now live, I live by *faith* in the Son of

God." John says: "This is the victory that overcometh the world, even our faith." Peter says: "You are *kept by the power of God through faith.*" Such is the philosophy of a holy life. Holiness is not simply a *state* of moral purity, but also the *result of right actions.* God makes us *pure*, but we are to make ourselves *holy*. "Blessed are the undefiled in the way, who walk in the law of the Lord." God's law is the *test* of character, the *rule* of life, and the *standard* of holiness. The gospel does not release us from *obedience*, but *purifies* our hearts and gives us *grace* to keep the law, so "that the righteousness of the law might be *fulfilled in us.*" If God has purified our hearts, we must purify our lives by abiding in him and keeping his commandments," or we will lose our purity and forfeit our pardon, and have to "lay again the foundation of repentance from dead works."

"Thou hast a few names, even in Sardis, which have not defiled their garments, and they shall walk with me in white; for they are worthy." (Rev. iii. 4.) Here, then, we have a few names held up by the great Head of the Church who "had not defiled their garments." It is here, during probation, we are to "wash our robes and make them white in the blood of the Lamb;" and so it is here, in a state of activity and trial, amid the temptations and pollutions of this world, we are to "keep ourselves unspotted from the world," and our "garments undefiled." Thus did the "few names at Sardis," and thus may all who are "born of God" keep themselves *pure*. It was this that made them "meet for the inheritance of the saints in light"—"worthy to walk with him in white." The whole life of such a Christian is fragrant with the odors of paradise:

> When one that holds communion with the skies
> Has filled his urn where these pure waters rise,
> And once more mingles with us meaner things,
> 'Tis even as if an angel shook his wings.
> Immortal fragrance fills the circuit wide,
> That tells us whence his treasures are supplied.

If the Church had the moral power of which holiness of life is the precursor, she might gird herself for the conquest of the world. Every member would then be transformed into a faithful Caleb or a believing Joshua, to sustain the uplifted hands of God's legates as they lead the hosts of Israel to battle and to victory, until a conquered world would join in the song:

> "Justice and mercy, holiness and love,
>   Among the people walk—Messiah reigns,
>   And earth keeps jubilee a thousand years."

Having "put on her beautiful garments," the Church would walk through the earth with the mien of an angel, while on every hand, as from the lap of spring, she would scatter the buds of hope to bloom in immortal blessedness. With a love as pure and quenchless as the ethereal fire of heaven, a zeal as fervent as the galvanic flame, a light as clear and stainless as the sunbeams; she would impart a sacred charm to the very name of religion that would cause the eager eyes of youth to look longingly forth, as the lark for the morning, that they might pour the sweetest notes of life's earliest song into the listening ear of heaven!

CHAPTER VIII.

"Not Under the Law, but Under Grace."

To unite faith and works, to harmonize the law and grace, so as to make a harmonious system of practical religion, is a work of vital interest to every Christian. To do this is to put the Christian on vantage-ground in developing a well-rounded character. It gives him such a view of the plan of salvation as will make him rejoice—rejoice though "with fear and trembling." Let no one suppose this to be a work of supererogation; for I know of no subject of so much importance that is so little understood. While it is possible for one to be saved in spite of doctrinal error, yet a clear view of the plan of salvation is necessary to the highest development of the Christian graces.

The love of God is the *source*, the death of Christ is the *meritorious cause*, and faith is the *condition* of salvation from the guilt and pollution of sin— that is, the plan of salvation originated in the love of God, there is no merit except in the death of Christ, and there can be no forgiveness and renewal of our moral nature without faith. It is exceedingly difficult to state and defend the doctrine of justification and sanctification by *faith only* without seeming to ignore practical obedience. To preach a *present salvation from all sin*, without "making void the law," is delicate work indeed.

Let us go back to first principles. Obedience is our *normal* relation to the divine government. All created intelligences are under obligation to obey their Creator. This obligation grows out of their creatureship, and runs parallel with their *endless existence*. No position we may assume to the divine government, in this life or the next, can release us from this obligation of obedience. So far from the saints in heaven being released from this obligation, their eternal safety grows out of the fact that they have been *confirmed* in a state of perfect obedience; and, instead of the lost in perdition being thereby released from obedience, it is this obligation that will kindle the flames that will enwrap them forever. So far from the impenitent sinner on earth being thereby released from obedience, it is this obligation unmet that involves him in condemnation already; and, instead of the justified believer being thereby released from obedience, he forfeits his justified state the very moment he willfully violates any one of the commands of God.

Practical obedience, then, lies back of the atonement, and can *never be repealed.* The design of the atonement was to put us where "the righteousness of the law might be fulfilled in us, who walk not after the flesh, but after the Spirit." The plan of salvation was introduced to meet the condition of man, not as he came from the hand of his Creator, pure and innocent, but as a fallen, guilty, and depraved being. In arranging this plan the question was not, How can man be released from all obligation to obedience? but, How can a guilty, depraved being be forgiven, and his moral nature "renewed in uprightness and moral purity," so that he can keep the law? Now, if it were possible for any sinner to keep the law from this moment until death, he would only perform his duty during that period of time, while all the "unpardoned past" would still stand against him. Hence, if his past sins are ever forgiven and his moral nature "renewed in the divine image," it must be done by some plan of mercy. The gospel is such a plan. Through the *vicarious* death of Christ God offers a full pardon for all past sins and a thorough "cleansing from all unrighteousness," upon the condition of faith only. "To him that worketh not, but believeth on him that justifieth the ungodly, his *faith* is counted for *righteousness*." "We conclude, therefore, that a man is justified by faith without the deeds of the law."

But what now? Is such a justified

believer thereby released from obedience? Is his probation at an end? Is the personal righteousness of Christ so imputed to him that obedience is no part of the condition of his *final* salvation? We will let Paul answer these momentous questions: "There is therefore now no condemnation to them which are in Christ Jesus, who walk not after the flesh, but after the Spirit. For the law of the Spirit of life in Christ Jesus hath made me free [not from the moral law, but] from the law of sin and death, . . . that the righteousness of the [moral] law might be *fulfilled* IN us!" Paul affirms that "Abraham's *faith* was imputed to him for [instead of past] righteousness;" that this "was written for our sake, to whom it shall be imputed [in the same way], if we *believe;*" that in this sense we are "justified by faith only," but that we are thus "made free from the law of sin and death," in order "that the righteousness of the law might be fulfilled [not in Christ for us, but] in us, who walk not after the flesh, but after the Spirit." Now this "fulfilling the righteousness of the law" is practical obedience; and this is what St. James meant when he said, "that a man is justified by works, and not by faith only," and "that faith without works is dead." Hence, that which St. Paul calls "fulfilling the righteousness of the law" St. James calls "justification by works;" and they agree in this: they both put this practical obedience *after* justification by faith only. Thus the seeming conflict between Paul and James is reconciled, and faith and works are harmonized so as to make a grand system of practical religion.

Now the only text which seems to conflict with this view is Paul's declaration, "We are not under the law, but under grace." Of all the "hard things to be understood in Paul's Epistles," and which "some have perverted to their own destruction," perhaps none has been so perverted as this—especially as this has been perverted to the destruction of good works. The truth is, the declaration, "We are not under the law, but under grace," can have no bearing on practical obedience or good works, unless it be assumed that the gospel has *lowered the standard* of obedience; but such an assumption would be Antinomianism gone to seed. Owing to the nature of moral law—it being "a transcript of the divine mind"—God could change his own immutable **nature as** easily as he could lower the standard of obedience. Through the *vicarious* death of Christ God can forgive the believing penitent; but if he could have lowered the standard of obedience **one** *iota,* then he could have released man **from all obligation to keep the law, and** saved his well-beloved Son from the agonies of the garden and the deaththroes of the cross.

What, then, did Paul mean by not " being under the law, but under grace?" Simply this: We are not under the law, or covenant of works, under which Adam was originally placed, **and in** which there was no provision for **pardon,** but we **are** under the **covenant of** grace which **was** provided for the express purpose of granting pardon. But **so far** from the covenant of grace lowering the standard of obedience, the command still is: "Thou shalt love the Lord thy God with all thy heart, and with all thy soul, and with all thy mind, and with all thy strength," and "Thou shalt love thy neighbor as thyself." Christ said: "If ye love me, keep my commandments." Paul said: "Yea, we establish the law;" and that its "righteousness must be fulfilled in us." And John said: "Little children, sin not—he that committeth sin is of the devil; but if any man sin, we have an advocate with the Father, Jesus Christ the righteous." Thus, while every believer is required to keep the law and live without sin, yet, in the event he sins, his case is different from Adam's in this: Adam was under the covenant of works which made no provision for pardon, whereas we are under the covenant of grace which was given for the express purpose of granting pardon; and this privilege of pardon is extended during our probation to the backslider as well as the returning sinner. But in either case this pardon is obtained not by works, but by faith in Jesus' name. Faith in Christ, as the atoning sacrifice for the sins of the world, is the only condition of forgiveness; and it is by faith that it might be by grace. If Jesus had "*paid all the debt we owe,*" as the Antinomians teach, then pardon for past sins and a release from all obligations to keep the law in the future would have been ours by right of purchase; for if "Jesus paid it all," the *whole debt is canceled.* In this view, salvation would not be of grace, but of debt; and not only grace, but faith also would have been excluded from the plan of salvation; for if the *whole* debt is *paid*, then all other conditions would have been superseded. "Jesus paid it all—all the debt I owe," may jingle very well as third-rate poetry, but it contains a false idea of the atonement as set forth in the Bible. According to the Scriptures, an atonement is not only a substitution of one *person* for another, but also the substitution of one *kind* of suffering for another. Hence Christ did not pay our debt in *kind or quantity;* * but owing to the dignity of his person and his relation to the divine government, when he took our nature and laid down his life for us, such was the *purity* of his life and the *dignity* of

---

* Christ did not suffer the *remorse of conscious guilt*, the bitterest drop in the sinner's cup of woe; nor could he have suffered *all* that was due the whole race. The idea is absurd.

the sacrifice and the *nature* of his suffering, God could offer *pardon* on the condition of faith, and *final* salvation on the condition of obedience. The atonement, then, is *not a commercial transaction*, in which God proposes to so impute the personal righteousness of Christ to me as to release me from personal obedience; but the atonement is such an expediency introduced into the divine administration as that "God can be just, and the justifier of all who believe in Christ;" and when the sinner is thus forgiven and "renewed in uprightness and moral purity," he is to seek grace through Christ, to enable him to keep the law. And if this is not done, he forfeits his justified state, and falls into condemnation; and having forfeited his pardon, he becomes responsible for the old debt that had been forgiven.

In proof of this I refer to the case of the unmerciful servant recorded in the eighteenth chapter of Matthew: "Then his lord . . . said unto him, O thou wicked servant, I forgave thee all that debt, . . . shouldest not thou also have had compassion on thy fellow-servant, even as I had pity on thee? And his lord was wroth, and delivered him to the tormentors, till he should pay all that was due unto him." Thus the man not only forfeited his pardon, but in so doing he became responsible for the old debt which had been forgiven. And that there might be no mistake as to what Christ intended to teach, he said: "So likewise shall my Father in heaven do also unto every one of you, if ye from your hearts forgive not every one his brother their trespasses!" But some one is ready to ask, Does not God say, "I will forgive their iniquity, and I will remember their sin no more?" Yea, truly; but we must remember that every woe pronounced against the sinner, and every promise made to the righteous in this life is conditional; and the contingency depends upon the voluntary acts of the creature, and not upon any change "in the Father of lights, with whom is no variableness, neither shadow of turning." Hence God says: "When I say unto the wicked thou shalt surely die; if he turn from his sin, . . . he shall surely live." And "when I shall say to the righteous that he shall surely live; if he turn from his righteousness and commit iniquity, all his righteousness shall not be remembered; but for his iniquity that he hath committed, he shall die." "Yet the children of thy people say the way of the

Lord is not equal; but as for them, their way is not equal."

Instead, then, of the personal righteousness of Christ being so imputed to me as to release me from personal obedience, I may forfeit my pardon by failing to forgive my brother; yea, Christ warned every man in the college of apostles of this danger. Hence, so far from it being true that the justification which comes to me through the merits of Christ being "eternal and unconditional," the Bible teaches that we receive this justification on the condition of faith, and that we retain our justified state on the condition of obedience. And so far from it being true that "if we are once in grace, we are always in grace," the truth is, a man may not only forfeit his justified state, but he may die in that condition; and dying thus, all his righteousness shall be forgotten, and he shall be punished for all the sins of his life. The Bible declares that "the righteousness of the righteous shall not deliver him in the day of his transgression." "When a righteous man turneth away from his righteousness and committeth iniquity, and dieth in them, for his iniquity that he hath done shall he die!" "If a man abide not in me, he is cast forth as a branch, and is withered; and men gather them, and cast them into the fire, and they are burned." "War a good warfare, holding faith and a good conscience; which some having put away, concerning faith have made shipwreck: of whom is Hymeneus and Alexander!" Thus we fear that hundreds who "were once enlightened and made partakers of the divine nature, and tasted of the good word of God and the powers of the world to come," have now "left their first love," forfeited their justified state, and are drifting toward the breakers where Hymeneus and Alexander made shipwreck of their faith; while others have left the "old ship" and gone to sea in the devil's craft, and as they sail on dreaming they are "bound for Canaan's happy shore," lo! it is a demon's breath that fills their sails, and a demon's hand that guides their bark to ruin. To every one who wants to save his soul alive in heaven the Bible says: "Christ gave himself for us, that he might redeem us from all iniquity, and purify unto himself a peculiar people, zealous of good works." "The blood of Christ shall purge your conscience from dead works to *serve* the living God." "He that endureth to the end shall be saved." And "Be thou faithful until death, and I will give thee a crown of life."

Thus we see that, instead of there being any conflict between justification by faith and justification by works, both are necessary in order to get to heaven. Justification by faith relates to the forgiveness of past sins, and must be repeated as often as we sin willfully. Justification by works is the result of retaining our justified state by "abiding in Christ and keeping his commandments." Now the Bible teaches that justification by works is the grand *basis* upon which the final judgment will be conducted. In every place where the judgment is brought under review, not one word is said about faith, but every man is to give an account of his works. "For we must all appear before the judgment-seat of Christ, that every one may receive the things done in the body, whether they be good or evil." "And I saw the dead, small and great, stand before God; and the books were opened: and another book was opened, which is the book of life: and the dead were judged out of those things written in the books, according to their works. And the sea gave up the dead which were in it; and death and hell delivered up the dead which were in them: and they were judged every man according to their works." "Behold, I come quickly; and my reward is with me, to give every man according as his work shall be!" "Blessed are they that do his commandments, that they may have right to the tree of life, and may enter in through the gates into the city."

The points discussed in this chapter are so vital, and a clear apprehension of them is so important to every one that would "work out his salvation with fear and trembling," we pause long enough to give a brief review of these points and the lessons they teach.

We learn, first, that *no sinner* can render acceptable obedience to God until he lays down his arms of rebellion, accepts pardon, and is "renewed in the divine image," by faith in the blood of the Crucified One. The persistent impenitent sinner is in a state of enmity against God; and so long as he occupies this attitude all his boasted morality and good deeds avail him nothing; yea, the Bible declares that "his ways, his thoughts, his sacrifices," and even "his prayers *are an abomination unto the*

Lord."* If the "righteousness of the righteous shall not deliver him in the day of his transgression," how can any act of the impenitent sinner be acceptable to God? "Your sword *first*, and then your hand," is the way for a rebel to surrender to his sovereign. "Let the wicked forsake his way, and the unrighteous man his thoughts; and let him return unto the Lord, and he will have mercy upon him, and to our God, for he will abundantly pardon." A man that has not been subdued by the cross is of necessity under the wrath of God. The atonement is a supreme effort of divine love to save man from the penal consequences of sin. The cross is God's final statement of the impossibility of winking at sin. The dying agonies of

---

*All this is equally true of a once justified believer who is now *indulging* any *secret sin*.

the Son of God demonstrate that sin can never be pardoned as a mere act of executive clemency—that *justice* is a supreme *factor* in the government of God—a consideration so vital that when Christ placed himself in the sinner's stead, even he had to *suffer!* Hence, if men will not be reconciled through the death of Christ, they must be subjugated by force. When any sinner has proved himself unworthy of a government of motive and moral suasion, he is degraded to the level of physical control; and, as a last resort, God maintains his authority by coercion and penal suffering. The atonement is a fact never to be repeated: it belongs to *probation*, and probation *limits* its provision for pardon.

We learn, secondly, that no justified believer can retain his justified state unless he "abides in Christ and keeps his commandments." But not every sin committed after justification is a sin unto death; hence we should not give up the struggle against sin, though we fall into sin again and again; for "if any man sin, we have an advocate with the Father, Jesus Christ the righteous," "who is touched with the feelings of our infirmities, and who ever liveth to make intercession for us."

We learn, thirdly, that for a sinner or a backslider to persist in sin, because the gospel is a grand system of forgiveness, is the very essence of ingratitude, the height of presumption, and shows a love of sin and a hatred of holiness which ought to make the cheek of a demon incarnate blush for shame. Yet there are more men and women going to hell on this line than any other. "Because sentence against an **evil work is** not executed speedily, therefore the hearts of the children of men are fully set in them **to do evil!**" **This is** the class "**who hold** the truth **in** unrighteousness;" "**and for this cause God sends them** a strong delusion **that they might believe a** lie, **that** they **all** might **be damned.**" **No man** ever rejects the offer of mercy without believing that he will have another opportunity of being saved. **Now** every sinner in **perdition** had his last offer of mercy, **but he rejected** it, **believing he** would have another; and in believing **that,** he **believed a** lie, and **sealed his** damnation.

Finally, as the grace **of** God is **the** *source*, and the **death** of Christ is the *meritorious* cause **of our** salvation, all who get **to heaven** will **join** in the **song,**

"Unto him who loved us, and gave himself for us, and washed us in his own blood, unto him be honor, glory, power, and dominion forever and forever. Amen!"

CHAPTER IX.
The Laws and Conditions of Spiritual Growth.

As it is now clear that the higher life is to be reached by growing in grace, it is important to understand the philosophy of moral development.

All vegetable growth is dependent upon extraneous influences—such as soil and sunshine, moisture and heat. No animal can live and breathe aside from air. The mind is dependent upon external conditions which must be supplied if vigor and growth are realized. So it is with our moral and spiritual natures. God can not be loved only as the attributes of his nature which awaken and call forth our love are perceived and contemplated by us. "We love him because he first loved us." The whole question of natural, moral, and gracious ability is too little understood. Such a thing as an agent acting wholly from his own center—as a self-centered and self-acting power—is not to be found aside from the Divine Being. There is a sense in which dependence is the condition of all created beings. This is one of the fundamental laws underlying their creatureship. "In him we live and move and have our being." The all-pervading Spirit is the conserving and sustaining life of our being. As in natural life we can not breathe without air, so in spiritual life God supplies all the necessary elements and conditions of such a state, so as to make virtue and holiness possible while he keeps us in bonds of obligation and in the sphere of dependence on him.

God requires no man to do without the ability to do; and this ability being given, or promised, it is left to man, as a responsible agent, to decide whether he will obey or disobey the divine commands.

To understand the laws of grace, so as to know how and where to take hold of them, is a question of vital importance. While all may be ready to admit that God is ready to perform his part, yet but few seem to have comprehended the laws of divine assistance so as to realize all that the gospel promises. How often does it happen that when we need divine aid we go searching in ourselves instead of making the effort and leaving the whole question of ability with God. The performance is our part; the power to do comes from God. It often happens that the ability is given as the effort is put forth. It was thus with the lame man who took up his bed and went his way, and the man with the withered hand who received the power in the effort to stretch it forth.

Thus the one talent becomes two by using it. As we go forth in the discharge of duty, our ability to do and suffer multiplies like the bread in the hands of the disciples. As they did not wait for the Master to multiply the bread before they began the distribution, but began with what they had, so we are to go forth to our work with our present ability, and God will give the increase as occasion demands. We must prove faithful to the grace already bestowed before we have the right to expect more. Thus the law of increase is found in the activity necessary to employ our present capital. Faith becomes strong by constant exercise. Love glows and burns in proportion to the labor it performs and the sacrifices it makes. So all moral powers live and grow just as they are "exercised unto godliness." The path of the Christian grows brighter as he advances. They who wait on the Lord shall renew their strength; they shall walk and not faint; they shall run and not be weary; they shall mount up with wings as eagles, and soar and talk with God.

If, then, you have but one talent, be sure to improve that, and in due time it will produce another. One talent improved is infinitely better than ten talents lying idle. He that improves that which he hath, more will be given unto him; while he who fails to improve that which he hath shall lose his original capital. Our final attainments depend not so much upon the number of talents originally given as upon the use we have made of them. What thou doest must be done quickly; for "the night cometh, when no man can work." Time is precious. Our interest for all eternity will be effected by what we do during life—during the little space of time that lies between us and the tomb. The foundation laid during our probation is the only foundation on which we can build forever. Let us see that this foundation is laid deep and broad.

We come now to consider the *conditions* of spiritual growth. If we are born of God we have already come under the first condition of growth. Spiritual life being engendered in the soul by the Holy Spirit, we are "free from the law of sin and death," and are ready to "walk after the Spirit" and to "grow in grace." Now this spiritual life, like all life, has the *law* of expansion, of growth within itself, as an inherent force. There is nothing that has life but what has such a law wrapped up in it. This is the nature of vital force wherever it is found. This distinguishes life from death. Death has no power of growth; it always tends to dissolution, but life always tends to growth. Thus the life of God, "the law of the Spirit of life," in the soul has a tendency to *expand*, to grow. All the babe in Christ has to do is to *comply* with the *conditions* of spiritual growth; the law of it being an inherent principle already at work in the newborn soul. If we do not grow it is because we impede the action of this law, just as some tribes of our race hinder the growth of certain members of their body by placing them in clamps. Under the appropriate conditions and influences which lie within our sphere of choice we should, on becoming babes in Christ, grow up unto men in Christ as surely as the child grows to be a man, or as the seed develops into the "blade, then the ear, and then the full corn in the ear."

We have but little to do with the *laws*, but a good deal to do with the *conditions* of spiritual growth. It takes a Liebig to analyze and classify the laws of vegetable life, but any peasant can raise vegetables enough to supply a village. So it might require an archangel to explain the laws of spiritual life and growth, but the simplest child of God may so comprehend and apply the conditions of spiritual growth as to become a mature Christian. Our spiritual life comes from God—"that which is born of the Spirit is spirit"—and he will keep it intact if we do not check the operation of its laws by allowing obstacles to be interposed.

In the parable of the sower Christ speaks of some in whom the seed did not bear fruit. "The cares of this world, and the deceitfulness of riches," "choke the word, and it becometh unfruitful." Christ here recognized the law of growth, and the fact that this law would have acted if it had not been *prevented* by "the cares of this world, and the deceitfulness of riches." These things prevented the law of spiritual life from "bringing forth fruit to perfection." We may permit thorns and weeds to grow up and choke the seed we sow, or we may keep these obstacles out of the way, leaving the seed to have free course to obey the laws of growth under which they are placed, and so "bring forth fruit" at the appointed time. So in spiritual husbandry the good seed will grow if we do not permit the energies and affections of the soul to be drawn off to nourish other and hostile growths. If the powers and affections of the soul are absorbed in other things, of course the divine life can not grow. It is as much impossible for it to unfold and "bring forth fruit to perfection" as it is for corn to grow and mature while overrun and choked with thorns and thistles. The soul must give itself up to the fruits of the Spirit, and let no intruder and usurper come in and occupy the sanctum which was "*swept and garnished*" when "the unclean spirit was cast out."

We may starve the divine life as well as choke it. Hence, another condition of growth is nourishment. A soul conversant with a few old stereotyped thoughts can never be the home of an expanding spiritual life. In such a soul this life, like every thing else in it, will be dwarfed. In such a soul religion may run into fanaticism, or quietism, but it can not shine out in its own native loveliness and beauty—"born of heaven and as free as the air."

Men of the world sometimes complain that the Church furnishes but few grand, well-rounded Christian characters. One reason is, the world furnishes such poor, dwarfed, contracted souls for the Church to develop. If the world will furnish great, generous, active, thinking, investigating minds for the divine life to grow in, then the

Church will show great, noble, living, and mature Christians. Another reason for this deficiency in Christian growth is found in the fact that the world is always busy trying to persuade or entice the members of the Church to leave the fountain of life and the bread of heaven, and come and sip of the cup of worldly pleasure and eat the husks of worldly comforts; and, alas! the majority of them yield to the temptation. Thus thousands have gone off after the world and are saying, "We are rich, and increased with goods, and have need of nothing;" and know not that they are wretched, and miserable, and poor, and starved, and blind, and naked! To all such the Master says: "Behold I stand at the door and knock; if any man hear my voice, and open the door, I will come in to him, and will sup with him, and he with me."

No one can say that his spiritual nature is starved for the want of an ample provision being made. For "there is bread enough in our Father's house" for all his children—"enough and to spare." We are not straitened and pressed in on all sides by our Father, but in ourselves. Our Father has made ample provision for the healthy development of every one born of God. But if we would grow we must feed upon this *bread of life*. We must drink often and deep at the fountain of life. If we would grow into the highest possible spiritual life we must gaze and wonder, love and adore, hope and rejoice—must ply our whole nature with the entire circuit of truth, stretch our cords on this side and now on the other, elicit our powers by all truth and beauty. To be a full-grown Christian, we must be developed heavenward and earthward—Godward and manward—linked to God and man according to our relations to each, and in harmony with both.

To attain the "full stature of a man in Christ Jesus," we must have a place, and take the time for meditation and prayer—some sacred retreat, where we may be *alone with God*. The most vivid moral impressions, unless often repeated, will, like the morning dew, be exhaled by the sun of worldly prosperity or brushed away by our necessary contact with the world. Hence the absolute necessity of retirement and meditation, as well as constant watchfulness against worldly charms. We must cultivate the habit of reflection, heavenly contemplation, and prayer. We must study God's word; bringing before the mind every day the great realities which the Bible reveals, and arrest them and hold them to the eye of the soul, and look at them till the impression is left upon our inmost nature—till the objects rise and stand out in their magnitude—till the effect becomes so fixed and incorporated that when we go out amid sensible objects we will carry the sanctifying influence of these things with us. Thus in the very business and bustle of life our thoughts would recur to the topics of retired meditation, and our worldly plans would be formed and executed under some just estimate of the comparative value of things temporal and things eternal.

It is said that in the Royal Gallery at Dresden may be seen a group of connoisseurs who sit for hours before a single painting. Then they walk around those halls and corridors whose walls are so eloquent with the triumphs of art, but they hurry back and pause again before that one masterpiece of Raphael. Lovers of art can not enjoy it to the full till they have made it their own by prolonged communion with its matchless forms. One could spend an hour every day for a year upon that assemblage of human, angelic, and divine ideas, and on the last day discover some new beauty and new joy. But what thoughts, what ideals of grace, can genius throw upon canvas like those great thoughts of God, of heaven, of eternity, which stand out in the purview of faith as the soul is *en rapport* with heaven? What conception can art imagine of the "Divine Child" which can equal in spirituality the conception which one has of Christ in the prayer of faith? How often do we say of a pleasure, "I wish I had more time, so that I could enjoy it to my heart's content!" But no enjoyment can be more dependent on time for its performance than heavenly contemplation and secret prayer. Hurried acts of devotion, to be of any value, must be sustained by other approaches to God, which are deliberate, premeditated, regular, and which shall be to those acts like the abutments of a suspension bridge to the arch that spans the stream. It will not do to lay such foundations in haste. If this be true in building a bridge, how much more so in building a Christian character! This thoughtful duty, this self-examination, this communion with God — how dare we to hurry through it as a childish sport?

The assimilating, transforming power of faith is clearly taught in the Bible and demonstrated in daily experience. This is true of every kind of faith. The whole nature follows the faith, and gravitates toward its object. We meet men in every community in whose faces we see avarice, lust, or conceit, as plainly as if written in words. They have thought and felt under the power of these qualities so long that they are made over into their image. "The Hindoo, who worships Brahma sleeping on the stars in immovable calm, comes to wear a fixed expression." The mediæval saints, who spent days and nights in contemplating the crucifix, came to "show the very lineaments of the Man of Sorrows, as art had depicted them;" and, in some cases, it is said that the very "marks of his torture were transferred to their bodies." Very early the faith of a man hangs out its label, and soon the whole man becomes a confession of its truth. A transforming process goes on: faith is the workman, and the *object* of faith is the pattern. The work begins within, down among the affections and desires, and the forces move outward until the external man becomes, in feature and expression, like the object of our worship. This power of faith, first to transform and then to reveal, is wonderful. But as faith never reaches its true sphere until it enters the *spiritual*, and never finds its true object until it reaches up to God, so its greatest transforming and revealing power is felt and seen in religious experience. Faith is the power of love directed by will; and as it works out so it works within, shaping all things there after a divine pattern. It is by this principle that Christ unites men to himself. He brings men to believe on him in order that they may become like him. When sin came, death came also; and the entire system began to work toward death, in body and spirit. Christ introduces a reversing power, and turns the stream of tendency toward life. This is no mystery, unless it be a mystery that one being should change another into his likeness, or bring him under his power. We can conceive of a soul so transformed into the image of Christ, so recipient of his truth, so in sympathy with him, so obedient to him, as to have little sense of yesterday or to-morrow, to care little for one world above another, to heed death as little as sleep, because he is so filled with the life of God; for it is the nature of spiritual life to assert its pre-eminence over physical death. It is toward this high state of spiritual life and development that Christ is trying to bring us—sowing in our hearts the seeds of truth and love and life eternal.

As we "grow in grace and in the knowledge of our Lord Jesus Christ," there is a united action of all the faculties of the soul: thought has more faith in it, and faith more thought; reason more feeling, and feeling more reason; logic and sentiment melt into each other; courage is tempered with prudence, and prudence gets strength and courage from wisdom. The law of the conservation of forces holds here as in the physical universe. This united action of the mind, this co-operation of all the faculties, this *equilibrium* of all the mental and moral forces of the soul is something far *higher* than the disjointed experience of the early Christian life, something far *beyond* a state of moral *purity or sanctification*, something that can only be reached by a *growth*. It is like the action of the Divine Mind, in which every faculty interpenetrates every other, making God one and perfect. Now this state of maturity, of perfection in a Christian is an intimation that he is approaching the Divine Mind, and getting ready to go and *live with God.*

When our growth in grace and spiritual knowledge is *normal* and *unchecked* by sin there comes a state of spiritual life called a *mellow maturity.* The Christian graces have ripened and the man begins to feel and act like God. His heart grows soft, he speaks more kindly, a rich autumnal tint overspreads his thoughts and acts. This state is sometimes regarded as bordering on fanaticism, but it is simply the moral and spiritual natures rising above the common walks of men. Something of the divine patience and charity and wisdom begin to show in him, and we now see why God made man in his own image, and gave him his life to live.*

Such are some of the *conditions* and *results* of spiritual growth. The life of God in the soul, with its law of expansion wrapped up in it—the removal of all obstructions to its growth, giving it a heart "swept and garnished" and a mind "free from the law of sin and

---

* The idea that such a state can be reached by a single act of faith is absurd; hence the absurdity of confounding sanctification with Christian perfection—purity with maturity.

death"—wholesome food, drawn from the word of God by prayer, meditation, and all the means of grace; and then giving it free action in deeds of mercy in daily life, where we meet so much to move our pity and to stir our energies.

Thus the divine life, like all life, has its God-appointed methods of development and conditions of spiritual growth, and he will not change or annul these conditions. We can no more grow in grace while we ignore these conditions than the child can grow while deprived of all the conditions of physical growth. But if we will comply with these conditions, we will "go on unto perfection."

From this stand-point we can see the beauty and force of the following divine instructions—viz., "As newborn babes, desire the sincere milk of the word, that ye may grow thereby." "Therefore, beloved, seeing ye know these things before, beware lest ye also, being led away with the error of the wicked, fall from your own steadfastness. But grow in grace and in the knowledge of our Lord and Saviour Jesus Christ." "For when for the time ye ought to be teachers, ye have need that one teach you again which be the first principles of the oracles of God; and are become such as have need of milk, and not of strong meat. For every one that useth milk is unskillful in the word of righteousness: for he is a babe. But strong meat belongeth to them that are of full age, even those who by reason of use have their senses exercised to discern both good and evil." "Therefore leaving the [first] principles of the doctrine of Christ, let us go on unto perfection; not laying again the foundation of repentance from dead works, and of faith toward God." "And he gave some, apostles; and some, prophets; and some, evangelists; and some, pastors and teachers; for the *perfecting of the saints,* for the work of the ministry, for edifying of the body of Christ: till we all come in the unity of the faith, and of the knowledge of the Son of God, unto a *perfect man, unto the measure of the stature of the fullness of Christ:* that we henceforth be no more *children,* tossed to and fro, and carried about with every wind of doctrine, by the sleight of men, and cunning craftiness, whereby they lie in wait to deceive; but speaking the truth in love, may *grow* up into him in all things, which is the Head, even Christ."

After all that has been said and written about sanctification, it is the *birthright of all God's children*—"*the base, the substratum of a grand Christian life.*" It is to be "cleansed from all unrighteousness," "by the washing of regeneration and the renewing of the Holy Ghost"—to be "created anew according to the [original] divine pattern in uprightness and moral *purity*." And Brother Wood says: "*Purity* is not a high state of grace, when compared with the *privileges* and *possibilities* in the divine life." Hence the sainted Fletcher said: "With me it is a small thing to be cleansed from all sin; *but O to be filled with all the fullness of God!*" And Paul prayed "that ye, being rooted and grounded in love, may be able to comprehend with all the saints what is the breadth, and length, and depth, and height; and to know the love of Christ, which passeth knowledge, that ye might be filled with all the fullness of God."

"Finally, my brethren, be strong in the Lord, and in the power of his might; . . . praying always with all prayer and supplication *in the Spirit.*" If we ask the Spirit to help our infirmities, enlighten our minds, elevate our thoughts, purify our desires, and intensify our faith, then every groan and sigh will be carried up and whispered by the Spirit in the ear of mercy, and soon the answer returns laden with the richest blessings of heaven. But if we would "pray in the Spirit" and enjoy his aid, we must seek to "know the mind of the Spirit," and then yield to his divine impressions. Wherever he leads we must be willing to go. Whatever he dictates we must be willing to speak or do. The desires he inspires we must pour forth in fervent, earnest prayer. Those who are led by the Spirit are brought into a large place. Those who are taught of the Spirit become wise in the deep things of God. And those who are faithful co-workers with him enjoy his aid in all its fullness. This aid of the Spirit accounts for those seasons in which we find our souls burdened with a mysterious agony of prayer. These intense groanings are given in answer to some former prayer for the aid of the Spirit; and now, when we least expected it, the answer comes, and as we talk with God we know what it is to "pray in the spirit!" In such seasons every nerve of the soul is strung to its highest tension; we pour out our hearts before God; we pray with groanings that can not be uttered;

then words flow apace, and we speak in strains to mortal ears unknown. Such prayer is weakness casting itself upon divine strength; infirmity leaning on the arm of Omnipotence, and the cry of the soul for the fullness of God. It is the "weary dove returning to the ark" of safety; the soaring eagle mounting upward till lost to all below; the flight of the soul to the bosom of God, and basking in the supernal light of ineffable glory. To "pray in the spirit" is something more than to utter words in the ear of God. It is the eternal Spirit taking hold of the eternal Father through the mediation of the eternal Son. It is Divinity in us pleading with Divinity in heaven; for "it is not ye that speak, but the Holy Ghost which is in you"—the "Spirit making intercession for the saints, according to the will of God, with groanings that can not be uttered."

A day of glory will yet dawn upon the Church; but before that day shall come the Church must travail in agony for the "*fullness of God.*" For this Christ groaned in the garden and died on the cross. For this he sent the Holy Spirit to take his place in the world, and to "abide with the Church forever." And now the Spirit stands pledged to help our infirmities; to take of the things of Jesus and show them unto us; to teach us how to pray and what to pray for—making intercession for us with groanings that are unutterable. He is ready to endue us with power from on high and give us tongues of fire—to shine into our hearts and give us the light of the knowledge of the glory of God in the face of Jesus

Christ. He waits to reveal to us the unutterable, the inconceivable, and the unheard-of things which God hath prepared for his children. He waits to illuminate our minds and souls with the dazzling beams of grace radiating from the Sun of righteousness. He waits to make the glory of God pass before us, and give us in beatific visions to see the ineffable splendor of the divine nature. He waits to unfold and apply the exceeding great and precious promises to our individual wants, and cause us to rejoice with joy unspeakable and full of glory. He waits to lead us on and on, until we are

>Plunged into the Godhead's deepest sea,
>And lost in his immensity!

CHAPTER X.

The Christian's Secret of a Happy Life.

SECTION 1. LOVE AND OBEDIENCE.

MAN was made to love and obey God. This was his peculiar function, his highest bliss, while in his pristine state of purity. To "love God with all the heart, soul, mind, and strength" was, and is, the sum of all his duties, the apex of all his happiness, and the culminating point of all his immortal longings. God is love. This is the secret of the universe. The whole creation swims in an ocean of divine love. Every law and relation is established in love. To have this love "shed abroad in our hearts by the Holy Ghost," and then to respond to its mighty harmonies, and to know its height and depth, is the great and final achievement. To love God is simply to put ourselves in accord with the ruling principle of the universe. Consider Christ as the incarnation of divine love, and we see at once why we are to "love him and keep his commandments." By his incarnation divine love was brought into humanity. This was the only method by which human and divine love could coalesce. Hence, "if any man love not the Lord Jesus Christ, let him be accursed when the Lord cometh."

The character of Christ stands up alone in the world's history. It is a fact the most pure, ennobling, and transforming in the whole range of human knowledge. "He is the fairest among ten thousand, and the one altogether lovely." One view of his crucified Lord revolutionized Paul's whole nature. Thus it has been with thousands. Such a view of the crucified one lifts man's whole nature at once; and, like every thing perfect or divine, the more we know of it the loftier will be our appreciation, and the sublimer will be the transforming results. Like the blue arch above us, the character of Christ rises as we rise, lifting itself up into unattainable heights of purity and moral grandeur. When we shall have studied his nature through endless ages, and shall have passed from one height of glory to a higher still, the highest summit that we shall ever reach will only give us a more enlarged view of his boundless perfection and infinite loveliness.

Christ came not to teach the doctrine of the fall, but rather to *redeem* a fallen race; not to teach the love of God, but rather to stand forth the *incarnation* of divine love; not to teach the resurrection, but rather to demonstrate it by his own resurrection and ascension. The necessities of man were beyond the reach of mere teaching; he needed more than information. The wail of humanity told that its disorder was more than a synonym of ignorance. Others had taught and theorized. Ages of talk had passed, but man's condition called for one who could *perform* what others had promised; one who could make *real* what others imagined; one who would not save by *teaching*, but teach by *saving;* one who would not give a *theory* of life, but *life itself*—a personal Redeemer, whose words were deeds—the deeds of a Being *mighty to save.* When he could say no more he unveiled the cross and let that speak; when his lips were closed, he opened his heart and spake in blood; when his life-work was ended he exceeded all in the utterances of his death. Silence, if you will, every other utterance of his wondrous life; throw a veil over every other act he performed; hide every other object in the universe—but let me see the cross, for it tells me that he is my all-sufficient Saviour. If you will, pull down the moon, seal up the stars, and extinguish the sun, but let the hill of calvary stand, for there I learn that infinite love agonized to reveal itself, and died to utter its fullness. But for this an ocean of divine love would have remained forever concealed; but it found an ocean-channel in the death-throes of the Cross, and now we read in crimsoned lines that "GOD IS

LOVE!" O divine love! The source of our redemption! The essence of all our happiness! The sweetest harmony of the soul! The music of angels! The quintessence of heaven! That which melts the hearts of men and reconciles the discords of earth! A heavenly exotic transplanted in the garden of a purified soul—a divine creeper which entwines for support around the cross!

We are to be satisfied with nothing less than such a manifestation of supreme love to God as will lead us to "serve him with a perfect heart"—to delight ourselves in him as the source of all our felicity, to find in him all our happiness, so that we can rejoice and solace ourselves in God as our exceeding joy. "If ye love me, keep my commandments."

SECTION 2. THE **PHILOSOPHY** OF RESIGNATION.

The will of God is the supreme good of all created intelligences. God has a right, an infinite right, to our entire submission. All sin, in its ultimate analysis, is a revolt of the will of the creature from the Creator. Here we find the tap-root of depravity, the jugular vein of the old man, and the spinal column of sin. Now it is reasonable that our restoration should begin where our ruin commenced—the remedy must be applied to the seat of the disease. The submission of our wills to God's will is not only right, but our happiness. Without this there can be no true religion in the heart; for it is implied in the very term disciple, and is a prerequisite to the right performance of every Christian duty. Therefore, in the economy of salvation, God requires us to submit to him, to his laws and providence, to consecrate ourselves, our bodies and souls, our talents and influence, our time and property—our all—to him and his cause. We are to do as he directs, suffer as he appoints, and move in the sphere he selects.

When we thus resign all into his hands then he becomes responsible for our happiness, so long as we keep all upon the altar and live up to our vows of consecration. The assurance to such a one is "all things work together for good" to him. Is not this a grand and happy life? All he requires of us is an entire acquiescence in and submission to his will—"not slothful in business; fervent in spirit; serving the Lord." No need of all this fear and complaint against providence; all this anxious "thought for your life, what ye shall eat or what ye shall drink; nor yet for the body, what ye shall put on"—all this is superfluous, not to say sinful. It is our duty to do as God directs, and "he will supply all our need according to his riches in glory by Christ Jesus."

The true Christian, therefore, is not weighted down with the distracting care of earthly things; for he seeks the kingdom of God and his righteousness first—first in point of time, in point of importance, and of interest—seeks them first all through life, knowing that all other needful things will be added. He gives to the poor, and thereby lends unto the Lord, knowing that he will repay a hundred-fold. He goes and works in the Lord's vineyard, knowing that whatsoever is right he shall receive. He serves his "Master in singleness of heart," knowing that he will supply all his necessities. Here is the philosophy of a holy and a happy life, as it was taught not by Socrates and Plato, but by the Son of God. The Lord is our defense, the Holy One of Israel is our refuge, and Omnipotence is pledged in our behalf. "He has sworn, and he will perform it, as for blessing he will bless thee." If it were necessary, he would make the universe tributary to our happiness; and if that would not redeem his promise, he would create ten thousand more worlds and make them all subservient to the same great end. But what is one drop of water compared to the ocean, a leaf to the sylvan forest, or an atom to the whole creation? Less still are all our wants compared to the resources of him who openeth his hand and satisfieth the desires of every living thing. Shall the mite desist from bearing its weight upon the earth lest it should give way beneath its tiny feet? or shall the animalcule be troubled lest it should not find room and sustenance in the mighty deep? Yes; let these things be, but let no man fear to take the Lord for his portion lest he should suffer in the end. If there is a scene on earth over which angels might weep, it is the distrustful care so often seen on the faces of those who are called the children of God. Yet how tenderly does Jesus rebuke our unbelief: "O thou of little faith, wherefore didst thou doubt!"

As God has promised not only to do his children good, but the greatest good; and as he looks to our eternal interest as being of more value than that of time, so he regulates every part of his providence with reference to our happiness in the world to come; and so it will frequently happen that there will be many things in this life that will be mysterious to us at the time. "What I do now thou knowest not, but thou shalt know hereafter." To carry out his plans, and to make good his promise, our Father has to spoil our earthly comforts and joys in order to increase those to be revealed in heaven. And often that which he sees will make for our happiness in the world to come will appear to us as the destroying angel of all our hopes in this world. Just as the child playing with his toys thinks it a death-stroke to all his happiness when his father takes him from them and puts him under a course of mental discipline, simply because the child can only see himself as ever remaining a child and retaining his fondness for boyish sports, while the father looks far beyond to the time when the boy will be a man, with a capacity to revel in the higher joys that glow amid the coruscations of a brilliant intellect; so our heavenly Father, when he tears us away from our earthly toys and puts us under severe discipline, looks far beyond to that blissful abode where an eternal weight of glory will be the feast of the soul.

It often happens that as the panorama of an unfolding providence passes before us we gaze in astonishment at these heavenly wonders; we strive to comprehend them; we look at them and ask, "What do they mean?" but no answer comes to our troubled hearts. The clouds roll up and off, and we shudder as the vision of his chariot sweeps by, because we do not see the hand that guides it. We are perplexed on every hand; we reason, speculate, and philosophize, and fall back entangled in the meshes of our own philosophy, and no light comes to our bewildered minds and throbbing hearts. We are left to walk by faith, and not by sight. But it shall not always be thus. At the present we only look through a glass darkly, and we must be content by knowing in part. The reason we think that so little has been revealed is because there is so much yet to be made known; and the reason that so much looms up in the far-off future which we can not comprehend is because there is so much already made comprehensible. Instead of being so much troubled about these mysteries that belong to the future, let us feed on that which is already made plain. We ought not to refuse to admire and study the worlds which the telescope brings to view because it gives us reason to believe that all we know of the material universe is as nothing compared with what is yet to be revealed. He that improves the present will be the better prepared to understand the future. The child must neither throw away nor neglect his arithmetic because he can not demonstrate a problem in Euclid. The desired knowledge is not withheld arbitrarily, but is dispensed according to a wise economy, as we are prepared to receive it and are able to bear it. There are some things in the plan of salvation which the angels desired to look into, but they were denied the privilege. The gratification of a mere desire to know might thwart God's designs concerning us and obstruct the development of our hearts. Our hearts must keep pace with our intellects, our faith with our curiosity, and our practice with our knowledge. There is enough made plain to guide us in the pursuit of more, and progress is the great law here as well as everywhere else. We are traveling on to the fountain of light, and in that light which makes manifest all these mysteries will be finally explained. If faithful, we shall stand at last on the mount of God, and, looking back, all will be luminous like a thread of silver light running down the mountain-side up which the hand of our Father has led us.

Shall we not be resigned to his will when he assures us that, whatever may befall his children, he will make it a means of augmenting their happiness during the rolling cycles of eternity? What though the history of virtue is a history filled with suffering; that many of its scenes are drawn in characters of blood; that persecution has often prepared her racks and kindled her fires; that men of purest life and strongest faith have pined in dungeons or wandered in exile; and that "others had trials of cruel mockings and scourgings—were stoned, were sawn asunder, were tempted, being destitute, afflicted, tormented"—what of all this, if Paul tells us that they suffered these things "that they might obtain a better resurrection?" Moses, in leaving the "treasures of Egypt, in suffering affliction with the people of God, and bearing the reproach of Christ, had respect unto the recompense of the reward; for he endured as seeing him who is invisible." How often have the sublimest virtues, the holiest affections been evolved under the influence of sorrow! How much has the world risen in importance, how much has the moral universe gained in goodness and glory by the afflictions through which the saints have been called to pass! Had the trial of virtue been dispensed with, had there been no such thing in the economy of providence as tribulation to the righteous, then the examples of Paul's "great cloud of witnesses" would have been lost, the field of moral beauty and heroism wonderfully circumscribed, and the most touching incidents of time would have been lost to the moral universe. Now, add to all this that "eternal weight of glory" which these "light afflictions shall work out for us," and is it not enough to lift up the heads that are bowed down and confirm the feeble knees, to suppress every murmur that rises in the throbbing hearts wrung and crushed with sorrow, to clothe the dying hour in the gorgeous drapery of immortal visions and hang around the darkness of life and death the glowing ensign of *eternal resignation*?

SECTION 3. CHRISTIANS FOR THE TIMES.

The duties and responsibilities of Christians are peculiar to themselves. They stand isolated in one sense from the mass of the people, and the influence which emanates from them gives tone to the popular movements of their day. They are the exponents of the gospel, the oracles that speak to a slumbering world, the guardians of pure religion. It is desirable to have a ministry who can logically sustain, clearly elucidate, and enforce the doctrines of Christianity; but the true power of the gospel is found in the holy lives of those who profess it, be they clergy or laity. The world fixes its standard of religion not so much by the Bible and pulpit as by the effect it produces upon the life and character of Christians. The preacher may expatiate Sabbath after Sabbath upon the blessings and influences of the gospel; but what will this avail if he is surrounded by a worldly-minded and time-serving and an unholy Church? Now if every minister could say to his people, as Paul did to the Corinthians, "Ye are our epistles known and read of all men," then the mouths of the gainsayers would be closed. What cares the infidel world for tenets merely stated and defended in a cold, dogmatic form? It is the life of a holy man, though there be but *one*, they dread more than all the force of eloquence and the deductions of logic. But "if the salt has lost its savor, wherewith shall the world be salted?" Nothing in the moral world is more useless, pernicious, and contemptible than an impure, worldly-minded, pleasure-seeking Church—useless, because it does not answer the avowed end of its existence, to purify the world; pernicious, because it corrupts the world; contemptible, because it is the *ridicule* of the world and the *disgust* of heaven. (Rev. iii. 16.)

The first business and highest vocation of every Christian is to "perfect holiness in the fear of God." The idea that a man's religion is a secondary thing is egregiously false, because it is based upon a low estimate of the end for which we were created. It is founded on the notion that a man's business constitutes his highest concern, that it is to occupy all his time as the source of his highest enjoyment, and includes all his duties. Now the very reverse of this is true. The divine command is, "Seek *first* the kingdom of God and his righteousness." "Whether ye eat or drink, or whatsoever ye do, do all to the glory of God." Religion should put its impress upon the whole character, expand and dilate every power, enkindle every element of sensibility, make every faculty tributary to its great end, until it becomes the master-principle to regulate every-day life and the true glory of man. Let this become the status of the Church, and who can estimate the results?

We need just now, in a peculiar sense, Christians for the times. In the providence of God the present generation is surrounded by extraordinary events and opportunities. During the last thirty years the civilized world has been in commotion. Sages and philosophers, scientists and theologians have gazed in consternation at a series of events so wonderful in their nature and so rapid in their succession as to appear in retrospect more like the illusions of fancy than scenes of real life. Owing to these upheavals, society is thrown up from its lowest depths; old lines of demarkation are gone; the obscure have come to the front; the masses are wandering in the chaotic fields of doubt and uncertainty. Thus thousands are drifting on these troubled waters, or driving into a darker sea at every plunge, and are anxiously looking for some beacon to guide them into a peaceful harbor.

We need, therefore, Christians of deep principles to sustain them amid the rage of this terrible storm; of burning zeal to stand along the breach of time as the light of the world peering far above the wreck that sweeps around, and throwing the light of the cross far out upon the surging billows, to guide these storm-wrecked mariners to the desired harbor. We need Christians who will ride upon the crest-wave of progress, rise upon the flood-tide of improvement, and keep pace with the adventurous spirit of the age, to mold and direct all for the advancement of the kingdom of Christ. We need Christians of deep experience and stern metal, who will ring out clear and strong upon the world, to call it to a pause in its mad career; men of pure hearts and powerful faith, who can stand like the storm-swept rock, the same amid the combined shock of winds and waves; of moral power to command our resources and direct our energies, arresting the proud monarchs of crime, the devotees of fashion, and the worshipers of mammon, and secure their allegiance to the King of kings and Lord of lords.

In connection with these stirring events a few scientists have made, and are still making, a fearful attack upon the Bible. These enemies of the cross are trying to capture the strongholds of learning and plant their batteries firmly upon the hill of science. At such a crisis every actor on the stage of life is an object of more than ordinary interest; for at such a time the facilities for doing either good or evil are fearfully augmented. The mind and heart of the devout Christian throbs with joy in the contemplation of the good he may do by "spreading scriptural holiness over these lands." Thanks to heaven, Zion's watchmen have already taken the alarm, while here and there a stripling from the ranks of the laity has gone forth with pebble and sling to meet these Goliaths of sin and Satan. The two hundred thousand converts of 1887 stand up as living witnesses of the fact that the gospel is still the power of God unto salvation. The tide of grace, which has already set in, will no doubt continue to flow until the universal Church shall be refreshed, and the reapers in the Lord's vineyard shall gather sheaves in all lands, and the rejoicing angels shout "harvest home!"

But before that day dawns the latent

energies and dormant powers of the Church must be baptized with holy fire and burning zeal. Instead of the kindling light she must have the glowing blaze, and instead of the gentle, permeating heat the volcanic shock and throes of fire and flame. It is the perfection of folly to expect success without these demonstrations of the Spirit. To think of conquering the world without them is as silly as to think of melting icebergs with moonbeams. Heaven sympathizes with a Church in travail; and for the birth of souls the whole creation groaneth and travaileth in pain together, with mighty throes, until the shout of a newborn world shall usher in the millennial morn.

CHAPTER XI.

"Now of the Things Which We Have Spoken, This Is the Sum."

THE Problem discussed and the conclusions reached in the foregoing chapters are of so much importance that we add a brief review. In regard to Mr. Wesley's theory of the divine life, we have much we would like to say, but not now. There are a few things, however, that must be said here and now. It is evident:

1. That Mr. Wesley believed in the "second-change theory of sanctification."

2. That his views of the distinction between regeneration and sanctification were confused. At one time he said:

"It is undeniably true that sanctification is a *progressive* work, carried on in the soul by slow degrees." At another time he said: "Certainly sanctification is an *instantaneous* deliverance from all sin." And on one occasion he said: "Perhaps I have an exceedingly *complex* idea of sanctification."

3. That there is not a passage of scripture which Mr. Wesley uses in describing the state of the sanctified that he does not, somewhere, apply to the state of the regenerated. All that he gives to the one he takes from the other; hence, according to Mr. Wesley, regeneration and sanctification are identical.

4. That Mr. Wesley relied on the (so-called) experiences of men for his "second change theory of sanctification," and not on the word of God; for

he says, "The Scriptures are silent on the subject. The point is not determined, at least not in express terms, in any part of the oracles of God." And it is a remarkable fact that some of the men upon whose testimony Mr. Wesley accepted the "second change" theory soon after professed a "third blessing," or change, which lifted them up "above temptations." Hence, the question is, not what men say they have experienced, but What does the Bible teach? what is the Bible theory of the divine life? So far as the "second change theory of sanctification" is concerned, Mr. Wesley has taken it out of the doctrines taught in the word of God, and left it to stand or fall upon the testimony of men. Is this the reason why those who profess sanctification as a "second change" differ from other good men and women in nothing except in "*testifying*?"

5. Mr. Wesley was led into the "residue theory of regeneration" by the Ninth Article of the Church of England, and this opened the way to accept the "second change theory of sanctification," upon human testimony, when "the Scriptures were silent on the subject." But as he changed his views on sanctification from saying it was a "*progressive* work carried on by slow degrees," to say it was "an *instantaneous* deliverance from all sin," so he finally *rejected* the "residue theory of regeneration" so far as to cut it out of the Articles of Faith sent over to America in 1784. And he so far abandoned both the "residue theory" and the "second change theory," in his sermon on "Perfection" in 1785, as to say not one word

about "inbred sin," and to say that "salvation from all sin is the *least*, the *lowest*, branch of perfection."

6. Mr. Wesley always gave a Bible definition of regeneration; and but for the fact that he felt bound, as an ordained elder in the Church of England, to teach the doctrine of her Ninth Article,* and for the fact that he was disposed to accept, without closely analyzing, any good man's experience, there is every evidence to believe that the "residue theory" and the "second change theory" would never have had a place

---

* Mr. Wesley says: "A serious clergyman desired to know in what points we differed from the Church of England. I answered: 'To the best of my knowledge, *in none*. The doctrines we teach are the doctrines of the Church of England—indeed, the fundamental doctrines of the Church as clearly laid down both in her *prayers, articles, and homilies.*'" (Watson's "Life of Wesley," pp. 76, 77.)

in his theology; or if they had crept in, he would have expunged them from his teachings long before he expunged them from our Articles of Faith.

We have said that Mr. Wesley always gave a Bible definition of regeneration. Here it is *in extenso:*

Mr. Wesley says: "The state of a justified person is inexpressibly great and glorious. He is born again, not of blood, nor of flesh, nor of the will of man, but of God. He is a child of God, a member of Christ, an heir of the kingdom of heaven. The peace of God, which passeth all understanding, keepeth his heart and mind in Jesus Christ. His very body is a temple of the Holy Ghost, and a habitation of God. Through the spirit he is created anew in Christ Jesus; he is *washed*, he is *sanctified*. His heart is purified by faith; he is cleansed from the **corruption** that is in the world; the love of God is shed abroad in his heart by the Holy Ghost which is given unto him. And so long as he walketh in love (which he may always do), he worships God in spirit and in truth. He keepeth the commandments of God, and doeth those things which are pleasing in his sight—so exercising himself as to have a conscience void of offense toward God and man, and he has power both over inward and outward sin, even from the moment he was justified."

Again Mr. Wesley says of the new birth: "It is the change wrought in the whole soul by the Almighty Spirit of God when it is created anew in Christ Jesus, when it is renewed after the image of God in righteousness and true holiness, when the love of the world is changed into the love of God, pride into humility, passion into meekness; . . . a change from inward sinfulness to inward holiness; when earthly desires—the desire of the flesh, the desire of the eyes, and the pride of life—are in that instant changed by the power of the Spirit of God into heavenly desires." "In a word, when the earthly, sensual, devilish mind is turned into the mind that was in Jesus."

"Well," says Mr. Wesley, "what more than this can be implied in entire sanctification? It does not imply any new *kind* of holiness. Let no man imagine this. From the moment we are justified till we give up our spirits to God, love is the fulfilling of the law. . . . Love is the sum of Christian sanctification. It is the one kind of holiness which is found only in various degrees in the believers who are distinguished by St. John into little children, young men, and fathers. The difference between one and the other properly lies in the degree of love."

Now the same love which is in the "Fathers" is in the "little children;" and if this "love is the *sum* of sanctification," and the love of the babe is the same in kind as that of the father, it follows that if the father is sanctified so is the babe; if the father is *pure*, the babe is *pure;* for the difference is not in *kind*, but in *degree*, and the degree depends not upon an *extra act* of cleansing, but upon *capacity;* and this difference of capacity between the babe and the father is the result of *growth*, and not the result of a "second change;" but in order for the babe in Christ to become a man in Christ, he must have not simply a "*second* blessing," but a "*blessing*" *every day*. But is the babe, the newborn soul, sanctified "*wholly*?" Certainly; for he has that "love which is the sum of Christian sanctification." Moreover, Mr. Wesley says: "'To forgive us our sins' is to take away the guilt of them; and to 'cleanse us from all unrighteousness' is to purify our souls from every *kind* and every *degree* of it." "If any sin *remain*, we are not cleansed from *all sin;* if any unrighteousness remain in the soul, it is not cleansed from *all* unrighteousness.'" (See Notes I., John i. 9, and Sermon XL.) But does this babe "go right on to perfection," without a "second *change*?" Certainly; if he does not "leave his first love" and "defile his garments." In that event he must "repent" and "confess," and be "forgiven" and "cleansed," just as any other sinner; and this has to be repeated as often as he willfully "departs from the living God." There is but *one* process in the Bible to get rid of the guilt, the power, and the pollution of sin, and that process offers a PRESENT SALVATION FROM ALL SIN, BY FAITH IN CHRIST, to all who will accept it on these terms; and he who is thus forgiven and cleansed is to reach the "higher life," "perfection," or "maturity," by "growing in grace and in the knowledge of our Lord Jesus Christ," by "abiding in Christ, and keeping his commandments," and by "walking after the Spirit" and "fulfilling the righteousness of the law."

7. It is clear that no little of Mr. Wesley's confusion and "complex ideas of sanctification" grew out of the fact

that he confounded sanctification with Christian perfection. Hence his original idea that "sanctification is a progressive work, carried on in the soul by slow degrees." Then, after he had discovered that "sanctification is an instantaneous deliverance from all sin," he confounded sanctification with holiness. This mistake was more natural than the other, because Mr. Wesley was a firm believer in the "doctrine of created holiness."* Now holiness, like perfection, presupposes moral *purity*, or sanctification; but as perfection is reached by a *pure* soul growing in grace, so holiness is the result of a *pure* soul *living* right—"fulfilling the righteous-

---

* A doctrine that has been the source of several errors running all through Methodist theology, and about which I shall have something to say in the future, *Deo volente*.

ness of the law." Hence, while moral *purity* is the result of a divine *act*, holiness in a moral creature is the result of *right action*—that is, God can make us *pure;* but beyond this he can not make us holy. Hence, the possession of all the moral faculties in a *pure* or a *purified* state, and the possession of holiness, should never be confounded any more than *purity* and *maturity.* Now Mr. Wesley made both these mistakes; and in so doing he had at times "an exceedingly complex idea of sanctification," and not a few of our modern Fathers and teachers are in this particular genuine Wesleyan Methodists— "Simon Pure." But they differ with Mr. Wesley in this: Mr. Wesley always changed his views when he saw his error;* but they, like the "law of

---

* He changed his views, but was too busy to go

the Medes and Persians, change not;" and, what is worse, they can not see how it was possible for **Mr. Wesley** to have done so! (*Ex vitio alterius, sapiens emendat suum.*)

It is a remarkable fact that Mr. Wesley had the moral courage to follow truth although it led him to *contradict* what he had already published. But few men thus *love* truth, and fewer still understand the *charm* truth has to such a man. Thus Mr. Wesley went on searching for truth and publishing his thoughts to the world, never dreaming that those who should come after him would adopt either the errors or

---

back and change what he had written and published on the subject. Dr. Bledsoe has shown that Mr. Wesley intended to revise his works, but finally he left this work of revision to those who should come after him. Is it not time this work should be done by the General Conference?

mistakes with which he started but outgrew and set aside; much less did he suppose that posterity would hold him responsible for errors which he had rejected by *contradicting* them. To set this thought clearly before the reader has been the one object we have had in view in arraying Mr. Wesley against himself; but in doing this we have also had some insight into the magnitude of some of the errors which he had *inherited* from the Church of England, the mother of us all. In religious doctrine inherited error, like inherited depravity, can only be overcome by the throes of a new creation and a baptism of *light* and *love*. This baptism we believe Mr. Wesley received, and the evidences thereof are found in our expurgated Articles of Faith, and scattered all through his later writings, but especially in his sermon on "Perfection," published only six years before his death and one year after he had publicly rejected the residue theory of regeneration by expunging the clause in which it was baptized into the Creed of the Church.

Now this sermon on "Perfection" is in such perfect accord with Mr. Wesley's "Notes on the New Testament," and with his definition of the new birth, and in such harmony with the theory of the divine life advocated in these pages that if we were to add it as the closing chapter, one who is not familiar with it would never suspect that its author had ever held the "residue theory of regeneration," or the "second change theory of sanctification," while not a few who are teaching both these "theories" would read the chapter without ever suspecting that Mr. Wesley was its author. For the present we take our leave of Mr. Wesley, but not without assuring the reader that our admiration of that great and good man has increased at every step in the investigation necessary to write these pages.

We learn from this entire discussion several important lessons:

1. That no state of grace can be reached in this life where our natural sensibilities may not be stirred and excited toward forbidden objects; but that there is no sin in this excitement, provided there is no concurrence of the will.

2. That while temptation necessarily implies the power to yield, yet the very laws of the mind which make a temptation severe to the young convert will

react in favor of him who stands firm for a long time.

3. That the perfection, or "higher life," to which we are called as justified believers is not the **result of a** " second " and separate act of cleansing, but it is reached by a true unfolding of our moral and spiritual powers, together with the integrity of character which is superinduced by a retroaction upon the activity involved in resisting temptation successfully.

4. That while development and progression may ever remain a law of our spiritual and intellectual being, yet when we have so subjected our entire being to the will of Christ that a state of perfect moral equilibrium is reached —when the moral strength and reflex influence which follows right action have reached a point that cancels the

same natural consequences of wrong action, so that we are "rooted and established" in the principles of righteousness—then we have reached that *holiness* and perfection which is required of us, and which is the exalted privilege held up to every believer.

5. That if God in his wisdom calls the justified soul into eternity as soon as he is regenerated, there is no necessity for a "second change" to prepare him for heaven; but being "renewed in the image of God" and "created according to the divine pattern in uprightness and moral purity," he, like the thief, may go directly from the place of forgiveness to the paradise of God, without having to pass through either the theological purgatory of Protestantism or the penal purgatory of Catholicism.

6. That the cause of so little holiness in the Church is because so many yield to temptation and live the most of their time in a state of condemnation—though they may not have renounced their original purpose to serve God; and that the conviction of inbred sin which professing Christians frequently have is not the remains of moral corruption left in them at the new birth, but the corruption resulting from wrong action after justification.

7. That the reason the best Christians who have ever lived have written the bitterest things against themselves is not because they were cleansed only in part at the moment of regeneration, but because they had reached a state in the divine life which enabled them to detect the slightest deviation from that law which requires truth in the inward

parts, the righteousness of which is to be fulfilled in us.

8. That many have had needless trouble from confounding temptation and sin, so that every time they felt any excitement of their sensibilities under enticement, they believed that they had sinned, whereas this excitement was the essence of temptation; while another class, accepting the doctrine of "sin in believers," have lived for years in a state of condemnation, dreaming that all was right, because they had not denied the faith, committing sin daily, but charging it all to the "old man" whom they intended to put to death by and by; and that nearly all total apostates from the faith come from these two classes of errorists.

9. That while the "perfection" herein defined is of necessity the work of

time, yet who can tell how soon it may be reached? The fact is, when we come to understand the philosophy of a holy life we see that it may be reached much sooner than most Christians suppose. If the reflex influence of the first wrong act was such as to pervert and corrupt Adam's entire nature, it is reasonable to suppose that if the young convert would resist and overcome every temptation from the moment of conversion, he would not be very long in reaching a moral equilibrium where the reflex influence of right action would overcome the force of old habits, so as to establish him in the truth and give him all the fruits of the Spirit and graces of the gospel. Is not this Christian perfection?

10. That while it is the privilege and duty of every one born of God thus to

go on unto perfection; yet, "if any man sin, we have an advocate with the Father," so that no one should give up because he is overtaken again and again, but take warning of the past, continue the struggle until he becomes rooted and grounded and established, so as to "abide in Christ and sin not;" and though this does not put the Christian beyond the reach of temptation, yet it increases his moral power to resist it, and augments the probabilities of his final salvation—nevertheless "let him that most assuredly standeth take heed lest he fall."

Finally, we learn that the true method of obtaining the "higher life," or Christian perfection, is not by "laying again the foundation of repentance and faith," but, "leaving the principles of the doctrine of Christ, let us go on unto perfection" "until we all come in the unity of the faith and knowledge of the Son of God, unto a perfect man, unto the measure of the fullness of Christ;" "that we henceforth be no more children but may grow up into him in all things, which is the head, even Christ." And now "as ye have yielded your members servants to uncleanness and to iniquity unto iniquity, even so now yield your members servants to righteousness unto holiness. For when ye were the servants of sin ye were free from righteousness, but now being made free from sin, and become servants to God, YE HAVE YOUR FRUIT UNTO HOLINESS, AND THE END EVERLASTING LIFE."

www.ingramcontent.com/pod-product-compliance
Lightning Source LLC
Chambersburg PA
CBHW021209230426
43667CB00006B/629